1. Atlas Mountains Morocco

Tacheddirt village in Toubkal region.

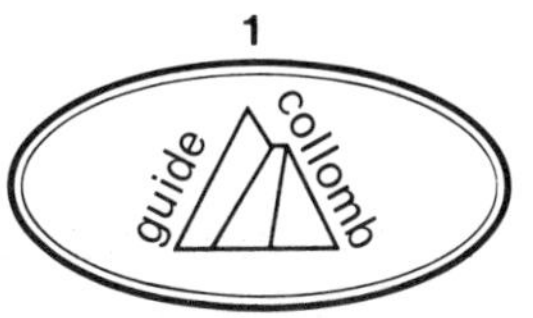

Atlas Mountains Morocco

ROBIN G. COLLOMB

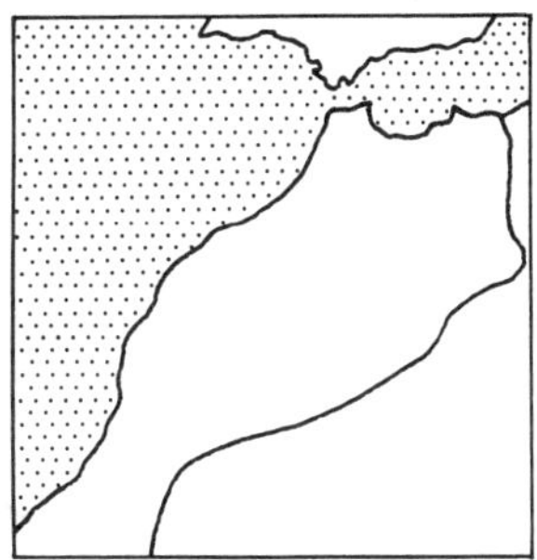

West Col

ATLAS MOUNTAINS MOROCCO

First published in Britain 1980 by

West Col Productions

Goring   Reading   Berks.   RG8 9A A

Copyright © 1980 West Col Productions

SBN 906227 08 9

Maps and drawings by Stephanie Collomb

Printed in England by Swindon Press Ltd
Swindon Wilts.

Contents

Illustrations

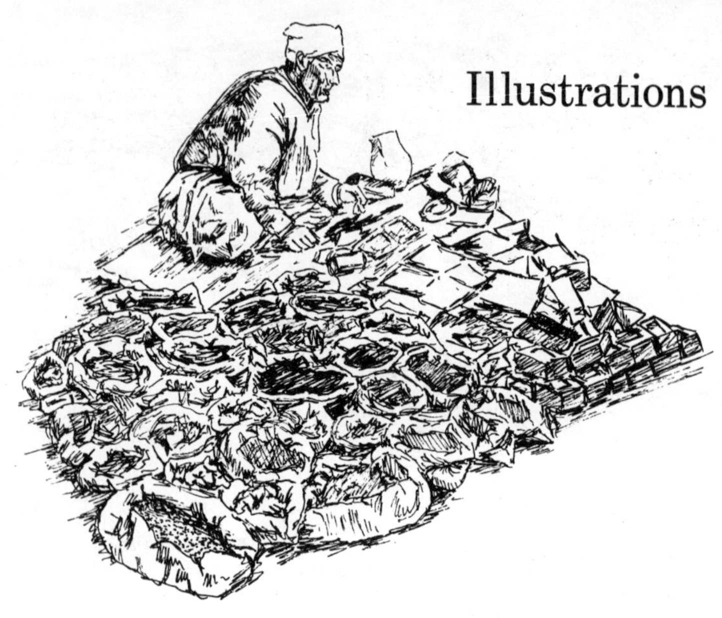

Tacheddirt village, frontispiece

between pages 56-57
Siroua 50 km. distant from Toubkal
Ait-Benhaddou
Imlil from road to Tamatert col
Toubkal north cwm
Panorama from Toubkal looking NE
Iferouane NW side
Neltner hut
Ifni lake from Ouanoums col (Mike Gibby, Henley)
Mizane upper valley

between pages 72-73
Toubkal from SW
Toubkal WSW ridge (Donald Mill, London)

Toubkal WSW ridge profile (Donald Mill, London)
Panorama of Aksouâl-Anrhemer chain
Toubkal south cwm (Donald Mill, London)
Ouanoukrim NE side (Mike Gibby, Henley)
Tadaft and Akioud E side (Donald Mill, London)

between pages 88-89
Ouanoukrim chain E side
Tadat N side (Frischer-Roberts Archives)
Bou Iguenouane and Adrar nou Ahior
Angour south face
Angour from Ouadi col
Angour from NW
Anrhemer from Angour

Photographs not credited above are from the West Col Archives.

maps on pages
Morocco, disposition of the principal mountain systems 8-9
High Atlas, selected roads and jeep tracks 60
High Atlas, Test to Tichka passes 97
Toubkal massif inner area 104-105
The last map is available full size, scale 1/100,000, as a sep-
arate sheet.

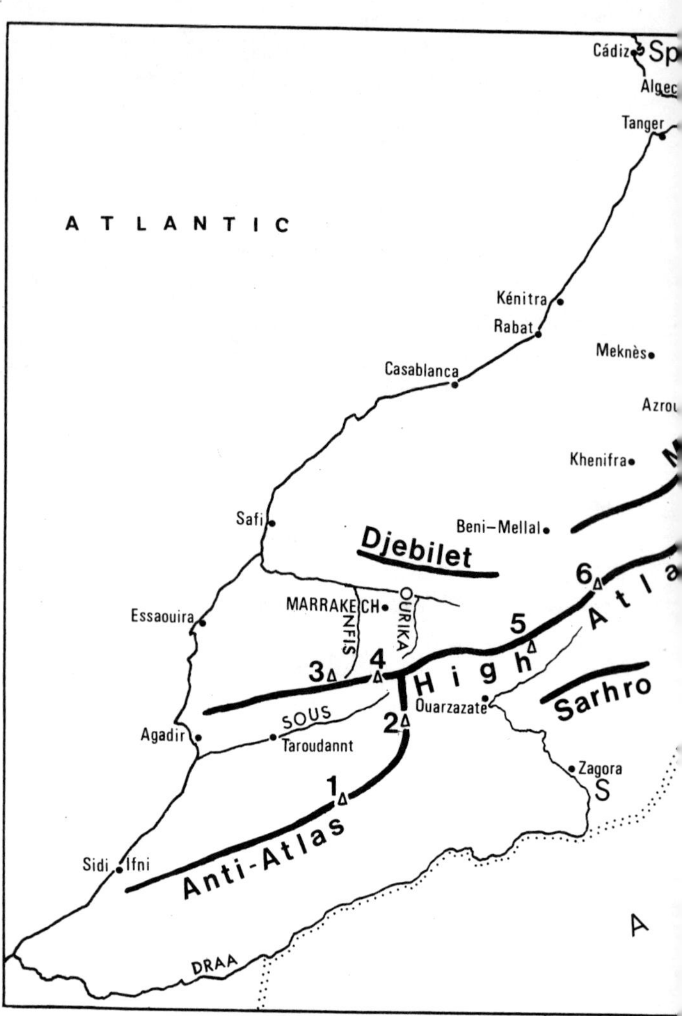

ATLANTIC
Cádiz
Sp
Algec
Tanger
Kénitra
Rabat
Meknès
Casablanca
Azrou
Khenifra
M
Safi
Djebilet
Beni-Mellal
6
MARRAKECH
OURIKA
5
High Atla
NFIS
3
4
Sarhro
SOUS
2
Ouarzazate
Agadir
Taroudannt
Zagora
S
1
Sidi Ifni
Anti-Atlas
A
DRAA

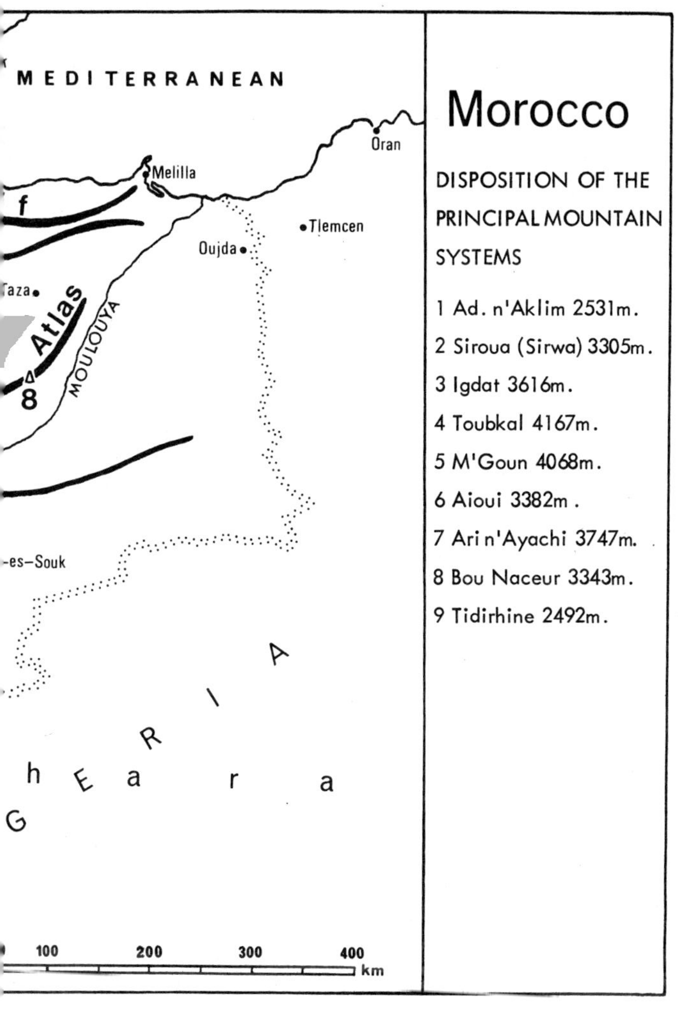

Morocco

DISPOSITION OF THE PRINCIPAL MOUNTAIN SYSTEMS

1 Ad. n'Aklim 2531m.

2 Siroua (Sirwa) 3305m.

3 Igdat 3616m.

4 Toubkal 4167m.

5 M'Goun 4068m.

6 Aioui 3382m.

7 Ari n'Ayachi 3747m.

8 Bou Naceur 3343m.

9 Tidirhine 2492m.

COMMON NAMES AND WORDS

Abid	Negro slave
Adrar	mountain
Afraou	(tafraout) artificial lake for water storage
Agadir	storecastles (for harvest)
Ain	stream source, pool
Ait	commune, village zonal group of people
Asif	stream, river
Assrdoun	mule
Azahar	lower winter pasture
Azib	pastoral shelter, hut
Ben	as Ait
Bou	possessive/genitive case for proper names
Ibn	son of
Idraren	mountain
Ifrane	(Ifri) cave
Irhil	mountain massif
Irhzer	ravine
Jbel	Djebel and other forms = mount(ain)
Kasbah	fort
Medina	native quarter of town
Moufflon	mountain goat or sheep, approximating to Alpine chamois; habitat 2-4000m., mostly above 3300m. Agile, sure-footed and similar characteristics to chamois.
Oued	river, watercourse
Ouggoug	crude barrage/dam of stones raised across a stream
Ras	head
Sahara	(Sahra) wilderness
Seguia	(sequia) water conduit channel
Shot	lake
Sidi	saint, religious chief
Souk	market
Tadat	finger
Targa	dam and water conduits for irrigation system
Tizi	pass, col

Introductory

POLITICAL HISTORY

Morocco, a kingdom since 1955 but traditionally the oldest independent sultanate in the Barbary States, is the one country of North Africa that benefits from a coastline spreading from the Mediterranean to the Atlantic. The physical neck of the African continent is severed only by the narrow Strait of Gibraltar from Spain and mainland Europe; consequently this has ensured a Spanish influence and partial occupation for centuries, while empire-building ambitions of other European governments have jostled for a foothold in the lands comprising Morocco for an equally long period.

Originally part of Mauritania under the Romans, the country fell under the Vandals in 429 but was restored to the Eastern Empire in 533. In 680 the Arab invasion began, and with little intermission the Arabs have ever since been possessors, if not always rulers, of the country, and the population is now among the most fanatical adherents of Mohammedanism.

At first, with Spain, part of the califate of Baghdad, it was not a distinct and united country till the beginning of the 18th century. Long afterwards it remained very backward and a passive resistance was offered to every improvement. Christian slavery, begun in 1650 and for which "recruits" were secured from as far away as Devon and Cornwall by dint of seaborne raiding parties, was gradually abolished and the mountainous interior areas began trading along caravan routes with the coastal plains. Even in the late 19th century the mountain zone was little different from what it was a thousand years ago, and many cities and districts were dangerous or impossible to visit.

By the Anglo-French Convention of 1904 the right of France to promote administrative reforms in Morocco was recognised and British political designs were withdrawn. Spain demurred but later made a private pact with France. Objections raised by Germany were discussed by a conference at Algeciras on the Spanish side of the "neck" in 1905-6, but incidents over German involvement continued for some years. French intervention to subdue revolts in 1911 led to the arrival of a German cruiser at Agadir - purporting to protect German interests but viewed as a manoeuvre of intimidation - and further strained relations between Germany and France. Ultimately Germany agreed to what was virtually a French protectorate of Morocco in return for a large slice of the Congo, and France concluded a treaty with Spain in 1912, acknowledging Spanish interests in the northern zone.

The Treaty of Fez more or less allowed the reigning sultan to pursue the spiritual leadership of the country while permitting the French to develop it economically, introduce social reforms, and to provide military security. This last function, aided by the Foreign Legion then at the height of its romantic reputation, consisted of waging a series of campaigns to pacify the interior mountain and desert tribes. The Berbers of the

High Atlas resisted to the last and only came under French control in 1934.

For over 40 years the French carried out sweeping changes in the administrative and economic life of the country, in which particularly roads and railways were constructed to the best European standards, and agriculture and new industries were developed so that today, for instance, Morocco is the third largest world producer of phosphates and the biggest exporter. Most of the benefits accrued to townsfolk living in the northern plains; the mountain peoples, steadfastly independent as ever, were bypassed by this economic growth, and those living in the Sous, to the south of the mountain barrier, down to the Oued Draa remained in poverty as before.

Following the rise of a nationalist movement against France, begun before World War II and given impetus and more confidence after the fall of France, the sultan Mohammed V Ben Youssef who had openly led the claim to sovereignty after 1949 was deposed in 1953 and exiled to Corsica then Madagascar. Increasing unrest and political pressure secured his return in 1955, whereupon he relinquished the absolute power that the sultans of Morocco had enjoyed for centuries (his Alaouite dynasty had begun in 1668), and became the country's first constitutional monarch (Mohammed V, 1909-1961). A cabinet and prime minister were appointed. Independence from France was recognised in 1956, and the ancient Spanish presence, including the international regime controlling Tangier, was conceded a year later. The present king, Hassan II, is the son of Mohammed V.

In 1979 about 40,000 French technologists, administrators, teachers and other professionals held important posts in Morocco, a reduction of 90% in 25 years. An active political faction, inspired by religious fervour, is intent on removing them. Most observers agree that this would have a detrimental effect on a country already beset by serious economic and social problems. While King Hassan II, whose portrait hangs in bars, hotels, shops and other public places throughout the country - reminiscent of the adulation expressed for Tito in Yugoslavia, holds the seat of power a reasonable level of stability is assured. He is in favour of retaining the French presence and connection, with their obvious benefits. But uncertainty and fear of the unsettling consequences that would follow his departure are uppermost in the minds of Moroccan intellectuals and the French alike.

PEOPLES AND RELIGION

Six principal groups inhabit the country. Berbers or Kabyles (Imaziren = free men to themselves) including Tuaregs, etc.; aborigines; Arabs; Jews; people of Spanish extraction; Moors or Arabs with an admixture of Spanish blood, though the name is often given to all the Mohammedan inhabitants; and Negroes. Traditionally the plains are occupied by Semitic Arabs and the mountains by Hamitic Berbers but many of the latter group are migrating north to the cities. The indigenous native population before all others is the Berbers, themselves consisting of various tribes, mostly of unknown origin. Jealous of their political liberty the Berbers opposed all the early invasions but could not resist the religious laws the aggressors imposed on them. The Berber idolaters were first converted to Judaism, then St. Cyprian preached the Christian religion. As indifferent Christians they practised every possible heresy, till in the 7th century Sidi Oqba (Okba), a companion of the Prophet, forced on them the Mohammedan faith. According to legend this heroic fanatic on reaching the Atlantic pushed his steed into the rushing waters and called Allah to witness that he would leave behind, from the Red Sea to the Atlantic, nothing but Mohammedans or corpses. Today some of the isolated mountain Berbers only pay lip service to Islam while the plains people remain uniformly devoted.

Morocco comprises the old kingdoms of Fez and Morocco and the territories found south of the Atlas chains - the Sous and Tafilalt (Saharan Morocco). While the last two remained independent all recognised the sultan as the Prince of True Believers, an office held by its bearer as the most powerful of the Sherifs or descendants of Mohammed. The sultan was one of the most perfect specimens of an absolute monarch existing. His so called ministers were simply favourites of the hour. He received the entire national revenue and spent as little or as much of it as he pleased. Every office was directly or indirectly purchased, small salaries or none were paid, the holders recouping themselves by plunder and oppression. All justice was bought and sold.

Owing to the religious fanaticism of the people, and the mutual jealousies of the European powers, the political equilibrium was preserved in Morocco for centuries. French occupation from 1912 gradually transformed autocratic practices, especially in the matter of local government, judicial affairs and administration of the koranic law to which all the peoples bowed.

Arabic, the official language, arrived with the religion of Islam, but the Berber tongues and dialects - an unwritten language that can be spelt phonetically - are older still and are widely spoken in the mountain regions. The southern Berber group, or Chleuh, lives in the High Atlas and in the Sous. All are Moslem. Berbers of the plain speak Arabic but the indigenous population elsewhere speaks Berber dialects (tachelhait). French continues as the language of business and commerce and is now widely spoken but rarely written by the mountain population.

Today the mountain Berbers are a racial group "hors taxe" in Morocco. That is to say they pay no revenues on income to the government and buy few goods or services from which the government collects a tax. It follows they receive no social benefits; moreover they ask for none. Independence from outside control and freedom to resolve their own destiny are fundamental to the Berber way of life. Even so the Moroccan authorities are beginning to intrude on this life style through local magistrates and their "caids" - a delicate and potentially eruptive step which if understood correctly will lead to real improvements for the Berbers - at the expense of some pride and monitoring of earnings. In practice, excepting isolated pockets of commercialism in agriculture and tourism, the Berber hill farmers earn no money. The wage for those who might leave the village farm to work locally say on a contractors' road project is £400 per annum. The majority live by trading goods and services between themselves and have no need of monetary transactions. In the last ten years the possession of money has become increasingly important and is seen by some as a means of reinforcing independence from authority. It follows that authority takes more interest in the Berbers when their purses fill up with banknotes. Those who may acquire currency have no banks in which to deposit it and use money to better their lot. An early priority is the purchase of a Moped to improve mobility in the countryside. Mopeds outnumber cars in Morocco by 500 to 1, even though mules and donkeys remain the traditional form of transport and haulage between settlements and markets. The Moped rider while not required to tax his vehicle, nor subject to any test or regulations, must find money for petrol which cost £1.60 a gallon in May, 1979, and was about to rise steeply as a result of another world petroleum crisis.

As people they are generally friendly and gentle, endowed with a high level of intelligence and sense of survival, but frequently squabble among themselves. Their grasp of foreign languages is remarkable and there is never much difficulty finding a Berber who speaks French, English or German, and some speak all three. The fierce belligerent character

ears ago hardly seems credible today.
largely a masculine one; males dress
urs - the instantly recognised garment
awn or grey burnous (hooded smock) -
children are best described as clad in
men work in the fields and do most of the
"supervise" or idle the day away gossip-
tend grazing animals, often at great alti-
their wares on muleback to other villages
traditional dagger in a girdle is mostly worn
on special occ   ions but the leather money satchel for those
in trade and business is conspicuously slung across one shoulder.

An outstanding quality of the Berbers is their fitness. This
follows naturally from hardy mountain people. Shod in poor
flimsy footwear they move over the roughest mountain terrain
like antelopes and could without trying outpace the strongest
and most athletic visiting mountaineer. Only a few years ago
their "sandals" consisted of strips cut from old car tyres; now
they seem able to afford more robust outdoor shoes while
cheap shorty Wellingtons are popular.

All Berbers are beggars by nature and the stranger is ac-
costed at every opportunity with a call or an extended hand for
"un Dirham", "un cigarette", or, from children, "un bon-bon".
Anything given to a Berber will almost certainly not be used or
consumed by the receiver, but exchanged with another for
something he needs more. The roadside is lined with out-
stretched hands clutching crystals and rocks for sale. Invitations to a meal of couscous and mint tea at some nearby house
are issued with monotonous frequency. Advice on resisting
these temptations is given in a later section of the guide.

In the last 20 years the tourist boom has spoiled the Berbers
and made them greedy. Outrageous overcharging is indulged
in until the visitor protests; he is then obliged to barter for

the best price obtainable. At its worst these negotiations become tedious, tiresome and frustrating.

PHYSICAL AND CLIMATE

Morocco is traversed by the several approximately parallel chains of the Atlas mountains from ENE to WSW, and spurs from these chains extend both to the coast country and the desert. In between there are numerous level plains, some of great extent and very rich. Most of the plains and plateaus have been denuded of timber and consequently look bald, with rolling hills and monotonous flats, green in spring, brown during summer and autumn. South of the Atlas, sandy wastes, long droughts - rain being scanty and uncertain, famines and the calamities of poverty are the prevailing characteristics. In western parts, though the soil is sometimes thin, actual desert is rare.

The central range of the Atlas forms the watershed between two drainage systems; one to the Mediterranean and the Atlantic, the other southward to the desert where the outflow is often lost in marshy sinks. Even the streams draining north are in a hot season or after long droughts little more than a succession of pools connected by threads of water - though rolling in brown floods during the wet season. An extensive system of irrigation canals (targa) serving field troughs (sequia or seguia) exists to serve the growth of crops and other economic needs, providing the mainstay occupation of the Berbers.

The climate in Morocco varies much. The western slope is tempered by sea breezes and protected from hot desert winds by the Atlas, so that it might be described as temperate. Temperatures seldom fall below 5°C or rise above 32°C. On moving inland the interior plains and valleys are very hot in summer; midday in the shade at Marrakech (Haouz plain) during August averages 42°C with 45°C not uncommon. Add 3-5°C for comparable temperatures on the south side of the Atlas. The average night-time temperature at Marrakech in August is 19°C. Retreating to the foothills and inroads to the High Atlas only brings slight relief; night-time temperatures at 3000m. can be as high as 15°C. July normals for 1600m. in the valley vary from 16° to 30°C (winter comparison, -6° to 12°C). Very little rain falls in the summer months and bad weather is confined usually to short but fierce rain or hail storms (sometimes snow) at 4000m. on the High Atlas. The crucial weather band is above 3600m. Even at this height weeks may pass before rain occurs; then temperatures in the early hours of morning are below freezing point.

Haze and cloud develop frequently in the mountains after midday in spring and summer, whereas in winter the atmosphere is often very clear during settled periods. A strong cold wind from the Sous can be an uncomfortable experience during spring and summer and may last for several days at a time. Best daytime temperature at 4000m. in July is 10°C.

Precipitation on the north slope of the Atlas is greatest between October and April - the Moroccan rainy season. It varies greatly - in some years comparative droughts are experienced, in others great floods result and rivers become impassable. November and February-March are normally the worst periods. The Atlas is capped by deep snow in winter and skiing has become a popular activity among the middle classes from the northern cities. Winter sports are now strongly encouraged by a national organisation for youth and student welfare. Snow settles down to 1400m. and in spring retreats to about 3000m. by mid May. From early July pockets of snow remain in hollows and gullies above 3000m. and by end August all traces of snow may have gone. These heights can be raised by 250m. after April for a drier than normal season.

FLORA AND FAUNA

The flora of Morocco is essentially European on the western

side of the Atlas. The fauna partakes of a similar character, the Barbary fallow-deer, wild boar, Barbary monkey, a species of porcupine and wild cat being the most prevalent mammals. A visitor could be forgiven for thinking that Morocco is overrun by the wild cat. The domestic cat, sleek and wiry, is in evidence everywhere. It mostly fends for itself, living in a pack, and is rarely taken into the house as a pet. The birds and fishes are those of southern Europe; of nearly 50 species of reptiles and amphibia known, half also belong to Spain. Moufflon roam the High Atlas and the eagle soars aloft. The splendid variety of birds in the mountain habitat dominates the wildlife scene. Moufflon are becoming wary and scarce due to the Berbers' persistent hunting instincts; the slaughter of ibex and chamois in the Alps 50 years ago is repeating itself. Scorpions and other insects in great numbers manifest themselves after May; they burrow under earth and stones up to a height of 3500m. The southern Moroccan scorpion, of which there are several varieties, is a nocturnal creature, emerging at night to prey on moths and other insects, and packs a powerful sting that could make some humans quite ill without speedy medical treatment. The voracious insect life infests mountain villages and in summer can cause the unsuspecting visitor some discomfort; the safest place to sleep is on the roof of a building - these being often flat. The mosquito is absent but replaced by a species of small fly which has a similar capacity for achieving bites through thick woollen clothing. There is no escape from them even at 4000m.

The ostensibly damp northern slopes of the Atlas allow the growth of a varied vegetation. Palm trees on the plain, olive trees to the foothills, walnut, cork and oak forests along the steep-sided inner valleys, superimposed by hardy conifers of pine and juniper reaching up to 2700m. A dry prickly scrub, a sort of porcupine thistle and painful for rock climbing, thrives to 3500m. where the landscape is already barren - analagous with the maquis of Corsica. Mountain camping is generally associated with thorny sites, and punctured tents and airbeds are a hazard. A pasture of grass for high camping so common in the urban European Alps is almost non-existent in the Atlas. In the numerous valleys where hillside scrub was previously taken as a matter of course for burning on campfires for cooking, combustible material is now conspicuously absent; a bad case in these days of conservation. While alpine-type flowers are not abundant, the thin remaining scrub blossoms in early summer to enrich an otherwise arid scene with multi-coloured strokes. The southern slope of the Atlas, facing the hostile super-heated winds of the Sahara, is nearly destitute of natural vegetation; those green patches seen are due to extensive works of irrigation.

ATLAS MOUNTAINS - GENERAL

Europeans attached the name Atlas to this the highest mountain range in North Africa in the belief that it was the home of the mythical Greek god. The Berber name is Idráren Dráren (Mountains of Mountains).

While reference has been made to a system of parallel ranges, this is only true in part while parallelism is more evident as sub-chains within particular sections of the system. Altogether the range extends from proximity to the highlands border plateau with Algeria in the east to the Atlantic in the west. The general axis is consistent and strikes ENE-WSW for a distance of some 900 km. At its greatest breadth along a line drawn between Meknès and Tafilalt it attains 300 km. For comparison with the Alps the approximate dimensions are 1000 km. and 250 km.

The most quoted phrase in all European literature - because it is so apt - comparing the Atlas with the Alps is a sentence from an article by Louis Neltner appearing in an issue of "La Montagne" (Paris) in 1929. "Il n'est plus beau ni moins beau

que les Alpes, il est autre" (It is neither more nor less beauti-
ful than the Alps, but something else).

In all this tremendous range we are primarily concerned
with a tiny section of the High Atlas merely 30 km. long and
situated about 70 km. distance south of Marrakech, the third
largest city in Morocco. The Toubkal massif (Adrar n'Dern)
is the most visited part of the range, having the obvious attri-
butes of great height and accessibility; it is now designated a
National Park (but as yet has no enforced regulations) and
boasts facilities comparable with "civilised" mountain areas
in Europe. A lot of earlier visitors, who up to the 1960s were
still able to enjoy a measure of original exploration and what
is popularly called today the wilderness experience, will regret
the transformation undergone in the last 20 years. This march
of "progress", recalling the tourist development of the Alps,
will undoubtedly continue and still owes some of its momentum
to the French influence. Before World War II hardly any serious exploration had been done in the Atlas mountains outside
the Marrakech zone. The lofty areas some 300 km. east of
the Toubkal region, approached from Beni-Mellal, Khenifra or
Midelt, only received close scrutiny by mountain explorers
(French) after 1948. But even these areas have now lost much
of their remoteness due to improved communications and the
advancement of tourism. Among these are the Masker chain,
regarded by many as the best skiing grounds in the Atlas and
visited annually by CAF organised parties; the Aioui cliffs
which provide the best rock climbing in Morocco, comparable
with the Dolomites for variety, difficulty and length; the Ari
n'Ayachi - simply the last big mountain at the eastern end of
the range, above Midelt, that everyone wants to climb. Along
the crest zone of the Great Atlas the distance between summits
exceeding 3500m. at one end and the other is 500 km.; they
number in scores and nearly all of them can be ascended by
"walk up" routes or on ski in winter.

22

Ignoring several prominent detachments, the Atlas divides into three principal chains. A main backbone, 700 km. long and called the Great or High Atlas, extending from the Algerian plateau to the Atlantic at Agadir. Then a parallel and shorter chain to the north, the Middle (Moyen) Atlas, with origins near Taza and petering out at Beni-Mellal after 350 km. Finally a huge wing detached vaguely at first from the Great Atlas watershed in the Toubkal neighbourhood, and soon rising to the extinct volcano of Siroua (Sirwa), which as the Anti or Lesser Atlas swings south then resumes a near parallel course with the main chain for 400 km. down to the Atlantic at the former Spanish enclave of Ifni. This last branch, an erratic and highly dissected upland plateau, is the least interesting, least visited and least known part of the Atlas system, being essentially a waterless desert range, though now traversed or partially followed by several motor roads.

Co-joined with the three main chains are the following. The Rif, a barren Mediterranean coastal range of little interest, but picturesque and a territorial barrier well known in Roman times, running in a bow-shaped loop from Melilla to Ceuta for some 300 km.; great limestone gorges and river defiles (Oued Moulouya) separate it from the northward end of the Middle Atlas. Then the Djebilet (little mountain) develops as an extension of the Middle Atlas, and reaching no respectable height passes north of Marrakech before fading out short of the Atlantic near Safi. Lastly the Sarhro, a distinctly more interesting massif, makes an isolated appearance on the south side of the Great Atlas and presents a 100 km. long frontage to the Sahara.

The predominant rock of the Atlas is Jurassic Limestone; terraced cliffs, huge escarpments, deep gorges and flat topped summits characteristic of this mountain rock are commonplace to the landscape. The calcareous heights of the Great Atlas are notably interrupted towards the western end by volcanic lavas, schists and quartzite, extending for nearly 200 km. from the Tizi n'Tichka road pass to the Moussa gorges, where the crest zone is already descending rapidly to the Atlantic. The Toubkal region is entirely composed of this volcanic series and the limestone is only seen at low altitudes. Austere and sombre in colour, and generally unsound, the lava rocks of Toubkal are among the most curious and unusual that a climber is likely to encounter. While volcanic rocks, and especially granite, are normally very hard, the Toubkal andesites and rhyolites are intensely fractured and bedded together as intrinsically loose masses. Naturally, in a volcanic series imposed on weathered mountains there must be areas of comparatively solid rock, and when this is found, perhaps on a cliff face or along a ridge, it tends to exist sporadically. The result in the Toubkal area is to find very steep rock walls with abundant but rather loose and oddly "powdered" holds. The jointed rocks seem to have a property of grinding together to produce with the red Moroccan desert dust carried in the air stream a removable layer according to season and conditions. Such texture of the rocks coupled with their grim aspect, tinted in all shades of red and brown but mostly looking grey/black, and colourless masses of scree immediately stamp the region with its most impressionable aspect for the visitor.

Scree slopes are the most memorable feature for those who frequent the mountains. The Toubkal screes are internationally notorious and are used as a yardstick for comparing similar slopes on other mountains. Some of the hardest words written about any mountain in the world appear in the Neltner hut log book at the foot of Toubkal. The fact is there are worse slopes, steeper and looser, on neighbouring mountains which are much less visited and therefore only known to the experience of a few. To avoid exhausting labour on these slopes the climber should visit the area in late winter or early spring when admittedly the weather conditions may be doubtful but snow can

24

be climbed instead. May is normally the last month for finding long runs of snow cover on the scree fields; the weather then is generally settled.

Rock climbing has its good and bad moments. The modern technician, festooned with his "nut runners" and other safeguards, will not be deterred by loose pitches if the climbing is interesting and sustained. Areas of sound rock do not necessarily provide rock climbs of the highest quality, and the guide endeavours to indicate the ridges and walls which are likely to prove attractive to the cragsman. More satisfying in the Toubkal region are the possibilities for snow and ice climbing, generally in long gullies which invariably are concluded with several pitches on rock in order to reach a summit. Ascents in this category are possible up to mid June, and in some places, such as the Tazaghârt NE face, all year round. In spring, when good snow can still be found, the area is noted for not having its ridges and rockfaces encumbered with awkward snow pitches. The rocks are usually snow-free. Thin snow bridges may however straddle gaps and saddles in rocky ridges, depending on height and location.

Surpassing all these considerations, the Atlas mountains - not least the Toubkal region - appeal most as mountain walking country. The range represents a touring and cross-country wilderness on the largest scale available within easy reach of western Europe. No allowance need be made for the Alps, where most of the areas and summits above 3500m. cannot be crossed by mountain walkers excepting those with real mountaineering experience. The same might be true of the Atlas during winter and early spring because of the deep snow cover. In late spring, summer and autumn all the ground is traversable by properly equipped touring parties but they also need to be kitted out for self-sufficiency and living rough in a way no longer necessary in the Alps where life revolves round a network system of huts, cableways and roads reaching to a great height.

Groups of 6 to 20 persons in organised tours, such as those offered by Treasure Treks, London and Eiselin Tours, Zürich, still account for over half the western Europeans, from many countries, visiting the Toubkal region. Most of these are mountain walking parties, a few are strictly climbers.

Some of the topographically significant summits of the Atlas system and its outliers are as follows:

THE RIF   Tidirhine 2492
               Tidiquin 2448

MIDDLE ATLAS   Bou Naceur 3343   Gaberaal 3290
                    Bou Iblane 3190

SARHRO   Amalou n'Mansour 2712
              Fengour 2516

ANTI ATLAS KNOT   Sirwa (Siroua) 3305

ANTI ATLAS   Ad. n'Aklim 2531

WESTERN HIGH ATLAS   Igdat 3616
Moussa gorges to Test pass road   Erdouz 3579
                                      Tinergouelt 3551
                                      Aoulime 3482
                                      Amzra (Oumzra) 3451
                                      Tichka (Imaradene) 3351
                                      Ras Moulay Ali 3349

TOUBKAL REGION AND OUTLIERS

Test pass road to Tichka pass road. This forms part of the
Western High Atlas and is examined in more detail hereafter.

CENTRAL HIGH ATLAS   M'Goun 4068
                                          Tignousti 3825
Tichka pass road to Plateau des Lacs   Rhat 3781
                                          Ouaougoulzat 3770
                                          Azurki 3690
                                          Anrhomer 3607
                                          Tiferdine 3542
                                          Aioui 3382
                                          Imedrhas 3319
                                          Koucer 3093

EASTERN HIGH ATLAS   Ari n'Ayachi 3747
                          Maoutfoud 3445
Plateau des Lacs to Midelt   Masker 3265

MOUNTAIN EXPLORATION

Throughout the story of exploration by Europeans it must be remembered that some of the main summits of the Atlas, including Toubkal, were almost certainly reached by Berber tribesmen in the course of hunting trips long before recorded ascents began.   For "climbs" by the natives there are no written records and little appears to have been gleaned from the memory of the mountain population by researchers. Indeed it was not until 1922 that the highest summit was assuredly identified as such.

The first Europeans to cross the Atlas were probably those taken into slavery during the 18th century. It is not surprising that the first to leave a record of a journey in the mountains came and went, like Lawrence of Arabia, disguised in native attire.   The Spaniard Badia assumed the name of Ali Bey and donned Muslim costume to penetrate the Atlas in 1804. Then French explorer René Auguste Caillé, returning from Timbuktu to Tangier after many adventures and misfortunes, crossed the Atlas in 1828 with a caravan that believed him to be an Egyptian. Needless to say these intrepid gentlemen spoke good Arabic.   In 1861-62 the German traveller Gerhard Rohlfs, again disguised, visited parts of the eastern Atlas, but speaking little of the language was unable to move about freely and rarely knew his whereabouts.

The first "official" penetration of the Atlas by outsiders came in 1871 when a small scientific expedition organised by J. D. Hooker was given permission to visit the mountains south of Marrakech - this of course being the then unknown Toubkal region.   In company with John Ball and G. Maw, the party eventually reached the Tizi n'Tagharât after local chiefs and guides had put every obstacle and delaying tactic at their command in the path of success. Hooker and Ball later reached a summit further west which appears to have been Erdouz (3579m.), although the height given by Ball approximates to 3475m.

German and French surveying parties began in some earnest to explore the range without making any notable ascents between 1880-84. Joseph Thomson was the next Englishman to gain access to the Toubkal region and he managed to attain the Tizi n'Likemt in 1888 - a very high scree pass furnished with a mule trail. This slow procession of travellers gathered little momentum before the end of the century; the pace quickened following easier access and slackening hostility from the Berber tribes.

Two Frenchmen, the Marquis de Segonzac and Louis Gentil, the second a noted geologist, commenced thorough explorations in which de Segonzac climbed Ari n'Ayachi in 1901 and Gentil came within an ace of reaching the top of Siroua in 1908. Both men continued their work into the 1920s which resulted in the mineral wealth of Morocco being exposed and developed on a large scale. The Moroccan section of the French Alpine Club was founded in 1922 and in that year de Segonzac climbed the Iferouane believing it to be the highest point in the range, only to observe the mountain now called Toubkal was distinctly loftier. An attempt on Toubkal in April the following year was rebuffed by fresh snow but de Segonzac and his party returned in June and got to the top. The height of Toubkal was determined in 1924 and a trigonometrical signal was raised on the summit in 1931.

After the conquest of Toubkal in 1923 new ascents in the region followed rapidly as French expatriate enthusiasm mounted. The ranks of the regular Morocco contingent grew to a dozen or more; among the leading lights were J. Balay, L. Neltner, M. de Prandières, A. Stofer, and above all J. and T. de Lépiney. From treading the summits by obvious ways, ridges and faces were tackled by a process of elimination from which a detailed picture of the Toubkal region was built up to compose the first maps of value to climbers. A second phase of French exploration in the 1930s produced the Tazaghârt north face couloir climb, which holds snow and ice all year round and is now the most famous and classic route of its kind in North Africa (J. Dresch, L. Fourcade, W. Othenin-Girard, R. Lévy, 1936). In the previous year Fourcade and Brondel had climbed the easier diagonal couloir in the same 650m. high wall. The north face couloir was descended on ski with three abseils in 1979.

In 1927 Bentley Beetham (1886-1963) arrived with G. Thomson. He was the only British climber between the two great wars to visit the Atlas regularly - about five times. His ascents of the Toubkal region summits with various companions are the first British ascents without exception. This interest in the Atlas, and in other esoteric places, is still not widely known among the climbing public, and Beetham is generally remembered for participation in the 1924 Everest expedition and as the man who opened up the potential for extensive rock climbing in Borrowdale (English Lake District) in 1945. Many unkind remarks were passed about him over the alleged manner he went about his Borrowdale exploration during World War 2, and the pity is that he wrote little about his more worthwhile contributions to mountaineering in the Atlas, Tatra and elsewhere.

The most amusing account of a journey to the Toubkal region in these early days emerges from the 1932 "Munich School" visit by A. Heckmair, G. Kröner and A. and F. Möhn. Having cycled from Munich to Barcelona, then locked up in a Madrid goal for a few days, the party proceeded "steerage" using the cheapest native transport available and by a roundabout route finally entered Marrakech. Here they passed the time (for their papers were not in order) dashing from one brothel to another, frightened for their lives, while the four weeks spent actually climbing were declared "interesting but not at all imposing". Their new ascents were not recorded in the 1938 guidebook. In the same year Andrea de Pollitzer-Pollenghi and his Italian companions M. Botteri and M. Dougan made an outstanding traverse of all the main Toubkal region summits over six days in August, amounting to 17 km. of ridge climbing. The international spectrum broadened when a Polish party consisting of Gronski, Kielpinski and Szczepanski appeared in 1934 and found a number of good face routes missed by the resident French. But there are acres of rock walls in the area and similar ascents continued up to the 1960s.

A landmark was established in Moroccan climbing in 1938 with the publication of the Toubkal area guidebook written by Dresch and J. de Lépiney. It was reprinted with some improvements in 1942. Compared with modern works of this type it seems less than perfect in its topographical assessments and descriptions. However we have to remember that Atlas mountaineering was still in its infancy compared with saturation exploits taking place in the Alps, and in any case the current outlook in such matters was still decidedly conservative. This guidebook, though now unobtainable except as a rare secondhand purchase, remains the standard reference work. The chapters on geology, flora and fauna, climate and vegetation, native life and workaday conditions on the land are models of their kind.

In 1979 a CAF official informed the writer that discussions are underway to have this guidebook reprinted in a facsimile edition, but that there is considerable opposition to the idea because the practical information is over 40 years out of date, and a new author should be sought to revise the guide completely.

A wartime Casablanca resident, Roger Mailly, pursued the work of exploration begun by his French predecessors and in five years acquired a unique knowledge of the Atlas ranges. In

1948 he discovered the Aioui cliffs near Zaouia-Ahanesal which attracted the attention of rock climbers in metropolitan France. They arrived in swelling numbers between 1950-53, among them two leading guides, Armand Charlet and André Contamine. New routes continue to be made on these great limestone cliffs nearly every year.

Exploration for ski-mountaineering possibilities in the Atlas was first carried out in 1942/3 by André Fougerolles, Robert Lacaze, Roger Mailly and others, which drew attention to the rarely visited massifs of Bou Iblane, M'Goun and Ayachi. The first "foreign" parties to ski extensively on Toubkal and in the Central zone including M'Goun, Azurki and Ouaougoulzat were Swiss - accompanied by Colin W. Wyatt - in 1949 and 1950. Much has been made since in articles and booklets about the uniqueness of springtime skiing opportunities "off-piste" in the Atlas; though undoubtedly attractive to the tougher breed of cross-country mountain skier, it has not captured the interest on a scale suggested in many reports and summer visitors continue to outnumber the ski-mountaineering fraternity by fifty times at least.

In the sphere of long distance journeys, the Englishmen Pennycuick and Thesiger broke new ground in 1955 by walking for 15 days in short stages from Telouèt to Za. Ahanesal in a traverse of the Central High Atlas. While this journey did not announce the trekking potential of the Atlas, it co-incided with the independent realisation that much of the terrain is ideal for similar if shorter tours that can be accomplished by experienced mountain walking parties.

Marathon traverses of the Atlas soon embraced the skiing fraternity and commencing in the 1960s several long winter and early spring expeditions have been achieved. The Scotsman Hamish Brown has made ski-mountaineering in the Toubkal region, outside the piste skiing and organisation of the Oukaimeden resort, a speciality peculiar to himself and his parties.

In the early 1970s a GR route (high level mountain walking trail) was mapped out by Michaël Peyron, from Midelt in the east to the Moussa gorges in the west, covering a distance on foot of 550 km. and occupying on average 30 days without rest days or diversions and variations to principal summits. Many variations are possible but most are restricted by considerations of shelter and provisioning.

The recording of new exploits and adventures in the Atlas is vague and haphazard - a welcome change from the lunatic extremes of British long distance endurance walks and technically labelled descriptions of rock climbing. It is hard to find reliable up-to-date reports in Morocco and readers of the bulletin boards in the Toubkal region huts will soon realise that no information on route finding has been posted since 1955-1960.

ROADS AND MOTORING

Main roads between large towns are constructed to a high standard for fast and safe motoring. Secondary roads in the mountain areas still have a good metalled surface but are considerably narrower. In particular most of the roads bordering, leading into or over the High Atlas are barely two-lane carriageways, and the following attendant hazards throughout the year should be noted.

Tarmac at the road edge is bare above a broken and rough hard shoulder. Large vehicles, such as lorries and buses, coming in the opposite direction force one to slow down and swing off the roadway onto the hard shoulder. Traffic moving in the opposite direction will do the same. Beware of driving too close to the tarmac edge which is often jagged and potholed.

Twisting mountain roads are notable for having no tunnels or cuttings. When the French constructed Moroccan roads this was an economy justified by the low volume of traffic and much of the argument holds good today. However this feature presents several unaccustomed problems for the European driver. Contouring the ground precisely results in frequent blind bends of 180°. On mountain roads these occur alternately as two or three double S bends together. The carriageway on these bends is often single lane with a wide hard shoulder for the other narrow lane - the latter normally being the descent direction. Other road users sounding off horns while negotiating these bends - sometimes continuous for several km. - does not assist driving concentration and contributes to frayed nerves. Moderate gradients are a mitigating factor. Roads steeper than 1 in 10 are rarely found anywhere in Morocco, and the main road passes across the Atlas rarely exceed 1 in 15. The average angle is about half that the driver contends with on wider roads in Europe and the Alps.

Fallen rocks constitute a common hazard, especially at night, while stones are thrown across the road where heavy vehicles have been driven for some distance along the hard shoulder. The situation changes from day to day. Precise details about roads in the Toubkal region are given in a later section of the guide.

More serious than any of the hazards outlined above is the danger presented by pedestrians and animals. Pedestrians use the roadway and hard shoulder for travelling considerable distances. Water conduits run alongside roads so that animals are taken there for refreshment and sometimes grazing. Herds of sheep, cows and goats are moved across the carriageway without warning, and great care must be exercised when these movements are sighted ahead.

Mules and horses are ridden or driven laden along the roads and outnumber motor vehicles many times over. It is a wise precaution to slow down when approaching and passing these caravans.

Even more serious are the following common occurrences. Many loose dogs roam the vicinity of roadways. They have a nasty habit of running after vehicles and barking ferociously. They seem able to distinguish between a "local" driver and a stranger. A dog gives up the chase only when it cannot keep up with the vehicle. If a dog paces in front of you, slow down until it runs to the rear, then accelerate away as quickly as possible.

Worse still are the games children play. While on their way to or from school, without warning two or three in a group will suddenly dart into the middle of the carriageway directly in front of approaching cars, gesticulating wildly and shouting, so forcing a driver to brake hard. These games of "dare" might be construed as training for the occupation described below, and the solution lies with the Moroccan educational authorities. At certain times of the day in country districts these events are likely to taunt the driver every 10 to 15 km.

The most common attempted interference with moving vehicles, which might occur every 5 km., are young men standing on the roadside with rocks and crystals for sale. The technique is simply to step out in front of a car, brandishing the object like a missile about to be thrown at the windscreen if you do not stop. Experienced Moroccan drivers use the device of driving slowly straight at the vendor, forcing him to jump back, then swerving slightly and moving off quickly. These roadside vendors are persistent and have developed a technique of forcing nervous drivers to draw up.

On the whole the pedestrian farming community using the road in company with their animals is considerate and careful in matters of safety. They expect you to drive slowly and a handwave in greeting and acknowledgement is exchanged by both parties. The behaviour of other road users is another matter. Goods vehicles, lorries and buses are consistently polite and show good driving manners - they always slow down and edge onto the hard shoulder. But many car drivers in the writer's experience fail to reduce speed and fly past you with a hair's breadth between vehicles. Driving by others on the wrong side of the road and cutting corners along hilly twisting sections is a danger the foreigner should be alerted to at all times.

Driving is on the right-hand side of the road. Roadsigns are numerous but often old and faded and difficult to read. Main junctions are marked in French and Arabic but secondary junctions in country and mountain districts may only be indicated in Arabic. Speed limits, normally shown in Arabic numerals displayed in the international convention, are posted on re-stricted sections of road and on the outskirts of towns and villages. The pace of driving in large towns is sedate com-pared with European cities, because of pedestrians, animals and Mopeds.

Nearly all secondary roads in mountain districts are unmade with a hardcore or dirt surface. Animals or vehicles moving along them raise clouds of red dust. Badly rutted roads are rare but large stones cause one to drive as in a slalom. The Berbers are forever manhandling obstructions off the road - not as a service to motorists but to protect the hooves of their animals.

Certain dirt roadways may become impassable at river fords, according to prevailing conditions, or for other reasons, while new jeep roads, such as that from Imlil to Tacheddirt, are often unwise journeys for ordinary cars. Although no warning sign is posted these roads may be prohibited to ordinary traffic. Always consult a trader or some official near the start of such roads before attempting them.

MAPS AND PLACE NAMES

Topographic maps of the Atlas and Morocco are published by a national agency in Rabat. There is no distribution of these maps anywhere in the country, and a personal call in Rabat is the only way to obtain copies. For some years West Col Productions has sold these maps in Britain which are purchased through an agency in France, but the import of stock is erratic and unreliable. Would-be postal purchasers abroad will find banks reluctant to draw funds to settle sums invoiced in Dirhams and a premium of 200% plus clearing agents charges are levied on small amounts. To emphasise the on-going availability situation with these maps, they are sold secondhand in Morocco for £6.00 or more per sheet at present.

All parts of the Atlas are to be covered in a new 1/50,000 and 1/100,000 series. Four sheets of the former fit over the latter. The 50m. series began publication first but now lags some way behind the newer 100m. series. While the 100m. series is treated in a more modern cartographic idiom than the 50m. series, it lacks a lot of detail in the mountain zones, being good on settlements and communications and bad in marking passes and summits. The highest point of a mountain is often omitted, spot heights are rare and not significant, names of passes and mountains are frequently missing and the location of many features is suspect - making due allowance for the map scale and thus some latitude for necessary approximation.

The 50m. series is better in many respects and depicts terrain in greater detail; however it is quite difficult to read because of the drab printing of contour lines and muddled areas of cliff shading. Rock features cannot be picked out easily or accurately as they can on similar maps of the Alps and British mountain areas. There are no alternatives for these maps.

A block of 4 x 100m. maps covers the entire Toubkal region. The adjoining sheets on all sides of this block have also been published. While the W side of the block includes the Tizi n'Test, the E side falls some way short of the Tizi n'Tichka, and the intervening ground must be covered by additional adjoining sheets on this side. Each map covers 48 x 54 km.

Sheet titles are as follows:

    top left   - Amezmiz
    top right   - Oukaimeden-Toubkal
    bottom left   - Tizi-n-Test
    bottom right - Taliwine

In the 50m. series the bottom left quarter of 100m. Oukai-meden-Toubkal is the key sheet. This extends from Asni on the left N edge, encompassing Oukaimeden, to the upper Ourika valley; down the E edge along the Ad. Mighiain, encompassing the Ad.-n-Dern, to the upper Sous stream at the villages of Issoual/Zaouite; the S edge extends about 3 km. below the Ifni lake, and the W edge comes up to include (just) Tazaghârt. This 50m. map is Jbel Toubkal, sheet NH-29-XXIII-1a. Issued in 1966, the adjoining sheets have not been published.

Smaller scale mapping, useful for planning longer trips, is conspicuous by its rarity or absence. Michelin maps of 1/500,000 and 1/600,000 are either no longer published or only available on a restricted distribution basis in France. An old grid series of 500m. maps published by the former French administration (IGN) and long out of print (last edition 1957-61) is scheduled to be updated and reissued by Rabat. If and when it arrives this will be a highly desirable map. Sheets of the International World series of 500m. maps (IWM) were pub-lished across Morocco fairly recently (1966-68) but dribbled out of print in 1979. Copies are already being sold at a prem-ium to collectors. It is an easy, pleasant and clear map to read, but positively out of date and lacking in much detail, e.g. does not even bother to mark and name the position of the Test and Tichka passes on their respective roads. The relevant sheet information is: Series 1404, sheets 420-C, 420-D, 453-A, 454-B (copies sometimes available from West Col Productions). Another 500m. series currently available is the Tactical Pilot-age Chart (TPC), a map mainly produced for and used by aviators. It is contoured at distant intervals and colourful yet seriously lacking in essential ground detail. Map for the Atlas is Series TPC, sheet G1-D.

Maps of a scale 1/1,000,000 are easy to obtain. The IWM sheets of this scale are poor compared with commercial productions although the latter are not contoured because they are primarily designed as road maps. Three are available in Britain in about 50 city and town centres from large stock-holding booksellers. They are all entitled Morocco and cover the entire country: published by Kümmerly & Frey (KF), Hallwag, and Michelin - sheet 169. The latter is best known but was out of print in 1979 for updating and reprinting. Some editions of this map to the present time have had selected sections of 1/600,000 printed within them, including one of the Atlas range between the Test and Tichka passes and containing a reasonable amount of additional detail.

Place names in the Atlas and Morocco have for many decades been translated into roman alphabet form which has remained fairly consistent; slight variations in spelling have appeared over the years but nothing has been introduced to alter instant recognition. All this spelling can be termed Frenchified arabic. Other forms of spelling, equally recognisable for a long period, are original names given by the French, probably because a native name could not be found, or simply because there was no suitable local name. Now another form of spelling has been introduced with publication of the new 100m. topographical maps described above. Half the names on these maps are changed from the traditional older forms, sometimes by a few letters which leaves the reader in little doubt as to the identity of the place or feature indicated, but often by a new name bearing no resemblance in our alphabet to the old. It seems that the Moroccan mapping authorities have decided to "Berberise" place names. Mindful that the Berbers have no written language, the phonetic spelling of the sounds uttered when the names are spoken by the inhabitants appears to read quite differently from all other printed roman alphabet forms. Howls of protest over the outrageous spelling adopted for the 100m. map have

so far fallen on deaf ears. The deed has been done and is unlikely to be modified.

To cope with this confusing situation, in the guide new names
are used where they resemble and can be identified with the
old, but where new names differ widely the old are adopted
with the new shown in parenthesis.

A regular convention for the use of hyphens and apostrophe
marks either side of the isolated letter "n" (= of) in place names
defies explanation; no two maps or publications use the same
form.   In this guide punctuation before the "n" has generally
been omitted in favour of a small space, while an apostrophe
is used after the same letter.

BIBLIOGRAPHY

There are no books in English, past or present, devoted to
the Atlas mountains. Since 1950 some thirty articles have been
published in various British mountain journals and magazines.
The literature of value to date has been published in French,
notably:

J. Dresch, J. de Lépiney. Le Massif du Toubkal. Rabat,
1938, 1942.

R. Mailly. Villes et Montagnes Marocaines. Rabat, 1964.

D. Dourron, M. Peyron. De l'Ayachi au Koucer - Randonnées
dans de Haut Atlas. CAF, Rabat/Paris, 1977 (presumed to be
the first volume of a series).

SEE ALSO

C. W. Wyatt. The Call of the Mountains, London, 1952 (two
chapters).

B. Clarke. Berber Village, London, 1959. An account of the
Oxford University Expedition to the High Atlas in 1955, including the Pennycuick-Thesiger journey referred to in the
historical notes above.

Many articles have appeared in French magazines, including historically important descriptions of exploration during the 20th century. Some impressive coffee-table picture books of Morocco have been issued by French, German and Swiss publishers.

Three or four general guides addressed to tourists in Morocco are published in English, but the best concise handbook is the Michelin guide _Maroc_, still only issued in French and widely sold in Britain. The French _Guide Bleu_ is the definitive work in this genre.

The famous CAF map of 1/20,000 published in two sheets in 1936, covering Toubkal and its immediate surroundings, can still be seen on the living room wall of the Imlil hut. At least 20 persons and libraries in Britain are known to have copies.

Practical Considerations

MOROCCO (Arabic - Maghreb-el-Aksa, "the farthest west") has a population of 18 million. Capital and seat of government is Rabat. Chief trading seaport, Casablanca. The largest cities are: Casablanca (in speech always called "Casa" in Morocco, pop. 1 million), Rabat then Marrakech (international code letters for all goods and services, MRT, pop. 250,000).

MARRAKECH is called variously the Imperial City, Red City (after the colour of its adobe rampart walls), City of the South (formerly the national capital when its common name was similarly "Morocco"). In keeping with other fortified settlements dating back to the early middle ages, Marrakech has a walled inner city (medina = Moslem quarter), and a modern European quarter (Guéliz) and industrial centre outside its walls. The central part of the medina consists of a maze of souks (markets), the largest of their kind in the country, a labyrinth nearly impossible to navigate without a detailed plan or a guide. A warning is that the market area is noisy and smelly, and perhaps not for the squeamish if you do not relish the sight of emaciated or sick animals; raw meat crawling with flies; a densely packed rustic kaleidoscope of humanity and squalor relieved by the undoubted craftsmanship of artisans' objects worked from wood, metals of many descriptions, ivory and all manner of materials. Jugglers, musicians, dancers, magicians, snake charmers and others are all thrown together in a seething jumbled scene. Unaccompanied tourists will be pestered incessantly by the Berber tradesmen and have their enjoyment ruined. Scuffles and fisty-cuffs are not unknown. Do not engage street-corner native guides who loiter in hundreds everywhere and dog the heels of visitors with uninterrupted chatter and pleading. Most of these men are agents for groups of traders in the souks. Official guides are supplied by the <u>tourist office</u> in the French quarter: Place Abdelmoumen Ben Ali.

Other large towns are: Fès (Fez), capital of the North and the original headquarters of the old French administration. Mèknes, situated near Fès, and famous as the headquarters of the Sultan Moulay Ismail during the 17th and 18th centuries. Tanger (Tangier), formerly the chief seaport of Morocco controlled by Spain then an international consortium. Agadir, the chief fishing port, devastated in 1960 by an earthquake resulting in 15,000 dead and many more made homeless. Rebuilt by the early 1970s, much of the former architectural glory gone.

ACCESS

Before the days of comparatively cheap air travel, the normal way of reaching Morocco was by sea to Oran (Algeria), Tangier or Casablanca. In the 1930s it became cheaper overland by train to Algeciras/Gibralter in Spain, then by the short sea crossing to Tangier or Ceuta. Motorists after World War 2 used the same route through Spain and crossed by car ferry. Now in the 1970s all these ways are more expensive than air travel, and those wanting a motor vehicle for touring the country can hire a car more conveniently than all the time, cost and trouble entailed in getting a vehicle to the country.

In 1979 scheduled air services from London Heathrow to Morocco operated two or three times a week, according to time of year, to Tangier or Casablanca (Royal Air Maroc/Air France, Boeing 727), with connecting flight to Marrakech. Journey time including aircraft changeover, $5\frac{1}{2}$ h.

There is a direct flight from Paris to Marrakech, but when starting from London you have to change airports in Paris - a considerable inconvenience in these days of frustrating movement and clearance through large international airports.

Tourist return airfare London-Marrakech in July 1979 = £225 (7 to 30 days ticket).

In 1979 there was still no APEX, ABC or economy fare offered by Royal Air Maroc, but a fare in this category now so widely available for overseas destinations seems likely to be introduced in the near future.

Marrakech Menara airport is situated 6 km. SW of the city. It has a frequent bus service, adequate taxi rank, and many self-appointed helpers touting for hotel business, etc.

The national airline provides a fairly good internal service between main centres in Morocco, though none of them is likely to be of interest for parties travelling in the Atlas. Small airports of possible value are those at Beni-Mellal, Ksar-es-Souk, Ouarzazate and Taroudannt. Private operators using Fokker Friendship or smaller aircraft fly a few times a week between these towns and Marrakech.

Morocco is not a scheduled destination within the European airlines' Fly/Drive scheme. Fly/Drive is operated in Britain for Morocco by Foreign Travel Ltd (specialists in all kinds of Moroccan package holidays but not in the mountain travel/ trekking field), 19-21 Bury Place, London WC1A 2JJ. Tel. (01) 242-2741.

For Marrakech four category/sizes of cars are offered for

one to three weeks for 2 to 4 persons, the charges being inclusive of return airfare by scheduled flights, all documentation
and insurance (collision damage waiver, extra - very expensive
- and do not be conned into personal accident insurance which
is covered by the London insurance), and a hotel night with
half-board on arrival, and similarly on the day before returning
home. There are no extras except tipping and petrol to re-
plenish the tank while touring the country. The cost for two
weeks for three persons in the smallest car offered (Renault
4) is little more than the tourist airfare. Rates for the same
Fly/Drive scheme starting at Casablanca or Tangier are 10-15%
cheaper. However, Marrakech is much the best base for
visiting any part of the Atlas mountains.

International driving licence is required for Morocco at present; obtainable from a national motoring organisation (£1.50
in 1979).

Passport entry visa is not required for British or American
subjects. No vaccination certificates are needed.

Medication for visitors to the Atlas. You are advised to take
salt tablets and a preparation (tablets) for water purification.
Mild dysentry and stomach upsets are common enough and pill
addicts should go prepared; for this Lomitol is the usual drug
but it is only available with a doctor's prescription. Asprin
for high altitude headaches are necessary for those prone to
this affliction - liable to be exacerbated in a semi-tropical latitude. Four thousand metres will feel more like 4500 to those
accustomed to the Alps. Insect repellent in a tube for smearing
on the body, or in an aerosol can for camping, should be taken
in the period June-September. A comprehensive portable first
aid kit should be carried.

Currency regulations forbid the import of Moroccan bank notes.
Any amount of foreign currency or travellers' cheques can be
taken into the country. This can prove inconvenient when

arriving late at night, although airport terminals are supposed to keep a 24 hours Bureau de Change service. Similarly hotels are authorised to deal with foreign exchange but may not be prepared to transact business out of normal working hours. In the mountains it is always better to have plenty of currency in hand because banks or reliable exchange facilities may be distantly situated. A receipt must be issued for all currency transactions, and these should be carefully preserved as they may be required by customs when you leave the country. These receipts must be produced in order to change any remaining bank notes into your own currency on departure. (If you do this at the last minute in an airport terminal you are likely to be offered only French francs).

The unit of currency is the Dirham, divisible into 100 units (called cents, but in fact, francs). Mid-summer 1979 rate of exchange, £1 = 8.00 Dh. US $1.00 = 3.92 Dh. The Dirham is not a currency traded on the international money markets, and in Britain for example you can neither buy the currency nor ascertain a market rate of exchange. The Financial Times quotes business rate transactions from time to time. In fact a free market rate of exchange, were it obtainable, would realise a trebling of value for nearly all "hard" currencies, including Sterling. The classical rate of exchange of the 1960s was over 30 Dh. to one pound Sterling. Consequently Morocco is not a cheap country for most foreign visitors.

<u>Insurance</u>. It is essential that holiday insurance covering loss of baggage, money and travellers' cheques, personal accident for most situations but not mountaineering, and medical/dental expenses should they arise, is taken out for a visit to Morocco. Most package tour arrangements and trekking holiday prices are inclusive of comprehensive insurance, and the independent traveller can buy similar insurance for about £9.00. Mountaineering insurance for accident, rescue and consequent medical/transportation costs can be bought in Britain for about

46

£22.00 (1979 rates).

Some indication of medical charges, etc. in Marrakech are as follows. Simple consultation/examination of 15 min., £6.00. Tooth extraction, £11.00. Prescription, two boxes of pills for three days, to damp down pain or an infection for an unserious complaint, £8-10.00. There are no professional medical services between Marrakech and the Toubkal region, that is to exclude a few quacks working among the Berbers. There is a scheme to extend medical work of a high standard among the Berbers but it suffers from lack of funds. Doctors are plentiful in Marrakech. A good dentist is: Jean Caillères, 112 Ave. Mohammed V (on first floor above the Café Négociant).

Small injuries and ailments like cuts and infected swollen limbs are common among the Berbers. They are rather careless when using sharp tools for digging and working the land. A visiting party is unlikely to come away without being called upon at least once to treat men with nasty looking wounds.

SERVICES AND REQUIREMENTS
Hotels in Marrakech and Morocco are classified in five categories by the star rating system. It is always hard to advise on hotels; there can be a considerable variation between similar categories in various parts of the country, and prices, while much the same within categories, influence choice more than services and facilities offered. Category 1 includes youth hostels and boarding houses (£2.00 bed and maybe breakfast). Comfortable accommodation with a good restaurant does not start below Cat. 3 (double room, with breakfast, £6.50 complete). In Cat. 3, European parties frequent the Hotel de Foucauld, Ave. El Maatib. Cat. 4, double room with bath, inclusive breakfast, £9.50. Cat. 4 and 5 hotels often have swimming pools. There are over 50 hotels in Marrakech to suit all pockets; consult the tourist bureau, see above (closed 1.00-3.30 p.m.).

<u>Public transport</u> by bus is widespread, generally good and comfortable so far as express services are concerned. There are much cheaper "country" services for the native population but these are hot, uncomfortable and notorious for bad time-keeping. At first glance there are no public clocks in Morocco, and half the population pays little attention to time.

Taxi services are reasonably priced; a party of three or four can travel painlessly from Marrakech to Imlil in $1\frac{1}{2}$ h. for £5.00 per head. An impecunious expedition of four with lots of luggage can clamber into an open pick-up truck and be transported thus for £2.50 a head, depending on your bargaining powers. Consult the tourist bureau in Marrakech for current timetables, bus departure points and fares.

For local services, the main bus station in the medina is beside the Place Youssef ben Tachfine (opposite the S side of the Koutoubia mosque - the most conspicuous landmark in Marrakech - its minaret is the only object visible for any distance when approaching the city across the Haouz plain). Buses may call first or later at pick up points in the French quarter.

At least four buses a day run to Asni and back. A similar service between Marrakech and Oukaimeden ceases to operate in the off-season from May to early July. This preposterous situation conflicts with one of the most desirable periods for mountain touring parties. See also detailed information about Oukaimeden during this closed season. At Asni there is a privately sponsored Berber taxi service in a Transit bus with seating for 10 or 12 persons, for going up and down the small road to Imlil at any time of day according to demand. The fare varies accordingly, with little opportunity for bargaining, and averages £2.50 for a one-way ride. This service can also be engaged for a journey to Oukaimeden over the scenic mountain dirt roads, sensational and tricky in places, past the Sidi Fars and Tadmamt holiday camp and Tizi n'Taslitane.

Regular bus service from Marrakech up the Ourika valley to

Setti Fatma, and an express service over the Tizi n'Tichka to Ouarzazate. There is no bus across the Tizi n'Test; buses stop at Ijoukak (entrance to Agoundis valley). Above this the road is rough and unmade. To continue to the pass a lorry can be hired in lieu of a taxi, and a similar service is available from Asni lower down.

<u>Provisions/foodstuffs/shopping</u> should be bought in bulk in Marrakech for transportation to the mountains. To adjust the ultimate weight that a high level touring party or any other group might expect to carry, limited provisions available at mountain centres and hamlets, in hotels and huts at valley level or higher, are indicated in route descriptions.

Do not try to buy provisions anywhere in the medina; you will spend hours arguing over prices. All shopping should be done in the French quarter. You need go no further than the long straight main road and business centre called the Ave. Mohammed V. About halfway down this on the N side is the covered French market with dozens of good stalls; an alternative venue is supplied by a small self-service store on the same side of the road at a corner in the out-of-town direction. Curious to relate there are no supermarkets in Morocco; the authorities prohibit them notwithstanding a special dispensation which allows this convenient form of western shopping to be found in Casablanca and Rabat. All shops are closed from 1.00 to 3.30 pm. There is no general restriction on the sale of alcohol and wines and spirits are sold in cafés, hotels and shops.

<u>Equipment</u> for the Toubkal massif or any other high area of the Atlas between March and early June should include for climbers crampons and an ice axe for all. From early July for the rest of the summer normal alpine climbing equipment can be dispensed with except for certain specialised climbs. An ice axe is always useful, one of 85 cm. as a walking stick,

or one of 65 cm. for climbers coming across a snow pitch in a steep gully. A hat with a wide brim is essential for protection from the sun. Goggles are optional in summer but sun glasses are helpful to reduce the glare. Sun tan oil or glacier cream also afford necessary protection, and lip cream will prevent a chapped mouth in strong winds. In winter and early spring climbers will need full alpine equipment, and skiers should go as they equip themselves for the Alps.

Toubkal has about as much respect paid for it as Snowdon has in Britain. Many ascents are made by persons in open neck shirts, cotton trousers and feet shod in plimsols or sandals. That quite a few fail to reach the top or lose the way and have to be shepherded down says nothing for commonsense and the publicity campaigns promoted constantly in the western world for safety and arriving prepared with proper equipment in the mountains.

Camping in the valley is indicated in descriptions. Mountain camping above 2500m. can normally be carried out freely. It is not easy to find level sites free from rocks and thorns. Cooking over open fires has become nearly impossible because of the shortage of scrub wood; it is tedious, anyway.

Portable cookers taken into the mountains are extremely useful for making all kinds of meals. Either carry gas cartridges and liquid fuel from Marrakech, or note carefully in descriptions where they might be obtained in the mountain areas.

Porters and mule hire, and the conditions obtaining, from valley bases are given in their appropriate places in the guide.

Mountain guides. About 30 Berbers have certificates issued by the CAF asserting acceptable qualifications for these men to act as guides. Beware of men coming up to you and offering their services as a guide - as many previous British reports testify the client will end up leading the guide. One of the approved men is the chief guide who has assumed the name of

50

Tensing - a better choice could not be imagined! He is reputed
to be first class and should be consulted, if not available himself, before any other guide is hired. He lives in a hamlet
near Imlil and can be summonsed if at home just as soon as
his name is mentioned to any bystander. The guiding day-rate
is about £5.50, food and possibly equipment to be supplied and
paid for by the client. Most of the guides now have mountain
boots, rather fewer ice axes, and fewer still crampons and
ropes. Any visitor willing to donate equipment to the guides
will be fêted. At present there is a dire shortage of small
day-sacks - virtually unobtainable in Morocco and fetching
prices like £30.00.

<u>Mountain rescue services</u> are completely informal in the Toub-
kal area. A rescue procedure manual is deposited in all huts
and huts are equipped with stretcher and first aid box. The
police, who may be some distance away, should be notified
eventually. Considering the mountains are densely populated
by Berbers, assistance is readily to hand. There are no telephones in the main valley bases, Oukaimeden excepted, but it
cannot be long before places like Imlil are connected. Telephone, police, etc. at Asni. A standby helicopter at Marrakech
airport can be called up at short notice in serious cases. There
is a modern French hospital in Marrakech.

<u>Organised mountain travel</u> and trekking tours are operated by
specialist travel firms from Britain and major cities in Western
Europe and the United States. The national Moroccan travel
agency or airline in various countries will supply details. In
Britain: 174 Regent Street, London, W.1. In the U.S.A.:
597 Fifth Avenue, New York, 10017.

<u>Inflation</u> in Morocco is running at over 20% per annum (mid-
summer, 1979), and this fact should be taken into account when
considering prices and charges given in the guide. If the rate
of exchange remains the same, costs will rise accordingly.

Valley bases Toubkal Region

Two motor passes cross the High Atlas either side of the Toubkal national park zone. On the E side the Tizi n'Tichka is followed by the P31 road from Marrakech to Ouarzazate; on the W side the Tizi n'Test is taken by the S501 from Marrakech to a junction with P32 (Ouarzazate-Taroudannt) some distance from Taroudannt. The Tichka road carries a fair amount of private and commercial traffic; the road is good though tortuous after Touama (Marrakech side) right across the crest zone to below Agouim (Ouarzazate side).

The Test pass carries very little traffic of any description. It is metalled on the Taroudannt side and finished as a dirt road on the Marrakech slope. Paradoxically the metalled side restricts the volume of traffic, being narrower and built with scores of hairpin bends. From the visitors' point of view it is quite illogical that this side should have been surfaced before the Marrakech which must be ascended many more times.

Both passes may be closed in winter due to snowfall. Open or closed signs are permanently displayed at various points, the highest having a warning notice with the words "barrière de neige", in a raised or lowered position.

<u>Tizi n'Tichka</u>   2260m. (2206m. on map, probably a misprint)

High pasture pass. Marrakech-col, 112 km. Col-Ouarzazate, 93 km. On the Ouarzazate side many touring parties and coaches make a detour to the village of Âit-Benhaddou to visit ruined fortifications and buildings on a hill above the river (see illus.) still occupied by Berbers in primitive living conditions. About 4 km. from summit on the Ouarzazate side is a turning E for Telouèt village (22 km.), which can be continued by a jeep road to Anemitèr hamlet in another 13 km., this being the roadhead and starting point for the fine but rarely visited Anrhomer group (3607m.). Before the Tichka road was opened the regular crossing point for caravans between the Sahara and the northern plains was the Tizi n'Telouèt (2530m.) whose immediate access on the S side is guarded by the village of the same name. Here is the stronghold of the Glaoui family that ruled this part of the Atlas and parried French advances with consummate political skill right up to independence in 1956.

Between the col itself (rough Berber inn and souvenir stalls) and the hamlet of Aguelmous are several good camping places and jeep roads winding W into the Bou Ourioul massif (3578m.) on the outer edge of the Zat-Ourika group. No services or provisions; care needed in using stream water here. Lower down the road on the Marrakech side is Taddert village (1650m.), with two small hotels, restaurants (one quite good) and ample provisioning. This is a more convenient base for parties without their own transport to penetrate the Zat valley and its surroundings.

<u>Tizi n'Test</u>   2092m.

Windy pass.   Marrakech-Asni, 47 km.   Asni-col, 87 km. Junction of P32 and S501-col, 37 km. Taroudannt-col, 89 km. While attaining no great height, an altogether more exciting though less scenic col than the Tichka, known and used since ancient times, jealously guarded by champions of religious doctrine and once considered impracticable without local know- ledge. A main trade and caravan route since the 12th century. Berber inn at last bend before top on Taroudannt side, and a similar inn at Ifni hamlet some distance down the Marrakech side. The col itself is narrow and restricted in all senses; the enclosed situation shuts out views which are better from points further down on both sides.   At the top a jeep road, barrier normally in raised position, mounts steeply to a television relay station (2543m.) where the views are excellent. No ser- vices. All the Taroudannt side is a narrow tarmac road of $1\frac{1}{2}$ lane width traversing steep slopes which make it prone to rock- fall. Continuous blind bends and a general feeling of exposure combine to make driving difficult; great care is needed on meeting traffic coming in the opposite direction. The gradient everywhere is moderate. On the Asni/Marrakech(Goundafa- Nfis valley) side the road is unmade but appreciably wider and more easily negotiated, especially at bends which are fewer and less fatiguing.   The road remains rough down to Ijoukak village; after that a good tarmac surface continues with some monotony in landscape to the pleasant vistas and cultivation of Asni. Ijoukak (1200m.) has two simple inns and limited provisioning. It stands at the entrance to the Agoundis valley, an important though rarely used inroad to the Toubkal region, the western end of the usual high level traverse done by discerning walking parties, and destined certainly to attain a position third only after Imlil and Oukaimeden as a popular base centre. At present there is a small hut supervised by the CAF at Ijoukak (see Huts section). Jeep road to Tarhebat (Taghbart) and the Makhzen mines gives initial access into the Agoundis valley.

Higher up the Test pass road and just before the constricted opening to the Ogdempt valley at Ifouriren (Mzouzit) hamlet is the Tin-Mal mosque, signpost on road for pedestrians, now in ruins and dating from 1156.   The branch valley mentioned supplies the main approaches to Igdat (3616m.) and Erdouz (3579m.).

More details of village centres along the Tichka and Test roads are given for the mountain areas just outside the Toubkal region in later sections of the guide.

ASNI, IMLIL AND THE MIZANE VALLEY

The much pounded trail from Marrakech to Toubkal. Outside Marrakech the S507 (garage) then 501 road is followed in long straights over the Haouz plain (animals and pedestrians) to Tahannaout (34 km., garage), then a twisting section through the Moulay gorge to a Berber watering place and market beside the river, and lastly a short stretch through a shady avenue of trees to Asni (1165m.) in another 13 km. Splendid outlook to the high mountain crests beyond. There are junctions to Oukaimeden before and just after Tahannaout, and at Asni, all described later.

Asni: garage, telephones, police station, postbox, taxi hire, variety of small Berber shops, youth hostel, one rough inn, one good hotel. More expensive provisioning than Marrakech. Frequent bus service from Marrakech in $1\frac{1}{2}$ h. (1 h. by car).

An Englishman has a house at Asni with sleeping for ten. Contact: R. Cleaver, Stirling House, 125-127 Alexandra Road, Farnborough, Hants., England. Grand Hotel du Toubkal, Cat. 4. Situated on main road beyond village and before turning to Imlil. Excellent French cooking. English spoken. Single, double and treble rooms with and without bath. 1979 rates: double with bath, Dh. 59.00 for two; treble with bath, Dr. 70.00. Breakfast, Dh. 6.00. Dinner without wine, Dh. 30.00.

Transit bus service from Asni to Imlil; runs according to demand at any time of day. On the main road a short way past the Toubkal hotel, turning L for Imlil. This begins as a good metalled road (no. 6038), fairly narrow, which runs for 7 km. before becoming a dirt road with a reasonable surface continuing for another 10 km. to Imlil. Infrequent and easy bends, ample width, no steepness anywhere. One of the most verdant valleys in the Atlas, the Mizane river supports a lively rural community, with cultivations and crops in evidence all the way up to Imlil (1740m.).

Imlil: no telephone, electricity or petrol, two or three small Berber shops (cubicles) with limited provisioning, one Berber inn, CAF hut. Porter, mule and guide hire services - stables and staging post at upper end of village. Car parking, Dh. 5.00 per day. Café service at Berber inn and one shop; meals served only by special request - either at café or in CAF hut. Some tinned food, processed cheese, sometimes butter, biscuits, cooking fat and camping gas can be bought. Always available: bread, powdered milk, eggs, fresh meat, rice, potatoes, tomatoes, fresh vegetables, fruit, lemonade, mineral water. No wines, spirits or tobacco. Beware of being sold old stock, and stale bread. Ask the price of everything before buying and compare with normal Marrakech prices. The Berbers will endeavour to overcharge two or three-fold. Take care especially over invitations to serve you with mint tea or a meal, e.g. couscous (the latter a sort of Lancashire hot pot cooked in a basin of semolina); these offerings may at first sound like a friendly gesture but extortionate prices will be asked afterwards. Examples of proper prices in 1979 are lemonade, etc., Dh. 2.00 per bottle; mint tea for four, Dh. 5.00; couscous for two, Dh. 12.00. Camping is seldom tried but practicable in fields with permission from an owner. Boil all water before drinking.

CAF Imlil hut: next to carpark, stonebuilt (1953), substantial and comfortable, small garden to sit in. Closely supervised by warden, father and son, living nearby. Places for 35 in

Siroua 50 km distant from Toubkal

Top: Imlil from road to Tamatert col, looking west at Adrar Adj (left), Mzic col and Jb. Tasghimout.
Bottom: Toubkal north cwm (Irhzer n'Ikhibi North) with NE ridge on L and upper part of south cwm route rising from right.

From Toubkal looking NE

OUKAIMEDEN

TAMADÔT
ANGOUR

TIC

3825

3728 S
3607

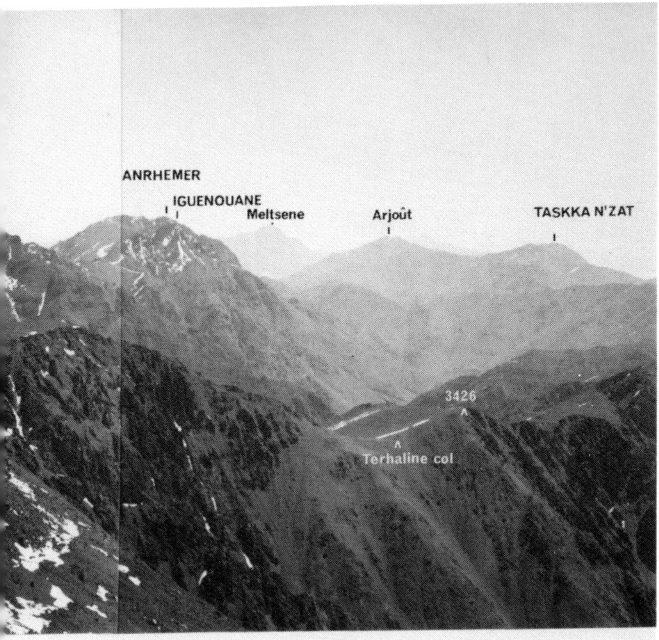

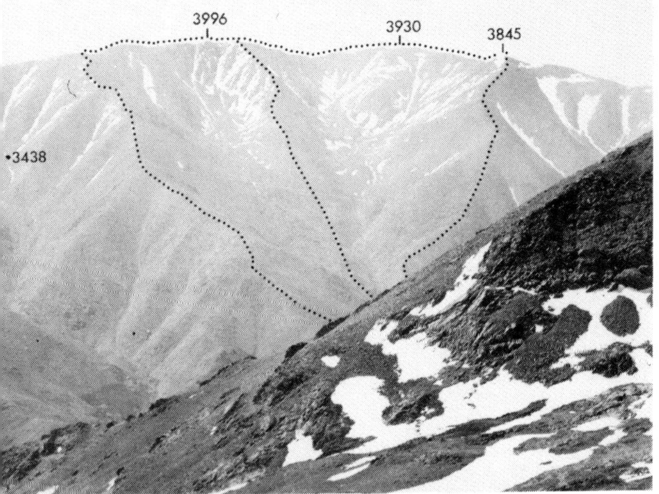

ANRHEMER
IGUENOUANE
Meltsene
Arjoût
TASKKA N'ZAT
3426
Terhaline col
IFEROUANE NW (Tifni) side
3996
3930
3845
3438

NELTNER HUT

IFNI LAKE from Ouanoums col

MIZANE UPPER VALLEY
BOU OUZZAL
3860
OUANOUMS COL
OUAGANE
col
3735
RAS N'OUANOUKRIM
4083
TADAFT
3900
E ridge roof
IMRHAZ RAVINE
IGLIOUA RAVINE
IKHELLOUN RAVINE
TADAT RAVINE
NELTNER HUT

separate bunks with foam mattresses in 4 rooms; no blankets
or sheets.   Large dining room and separate kitchen fully
equipped with all necessary pans and utensils; gas stove with
four rings. Running cold water in kitchen and in wash room
with 4 basins, shower cubicle and inside flushing toilet - when
it is working. Lighting by calor gas mantle or candles. No
extra charge for using kitchen facilities. Payment is expected
in the form of a gratuity for any task or work done by the ward-
en on behalf of a party, e. g. you do your own washing up or
must expect to be charged for it.

Hut rates, applicable for any establishment in this category
in the region, during 1979: members of the CAF and similar
national bodies having reciprocal rights (alpine system) including the Alpine Club, London, Dh. 5. 00 per night. Strict
examination of current membership cards is enforced. Slightly
higher rate for FFM and some other intermediate organis-
ations, e.g. professional guides and trade association affiliates.
All others without cards, Dh. 12. 00 per night.   Day rate -
staying in hut and using its facilities roughly from 11. 00 am.
to 5. 00 pm. - allcomers, Dh. 2. 00.

Porters and mule hire. Rates are fixed annually by the caid
at Tahannaout, and are posted on a noticeboard in the carpark.
Cynics declare that this board is allowed to become unreadable
so that the mulemen and porters can fix their own charges.
Among the malpractices are middlemen claiming an "agent's
fee" (Dh. 2-5. 00) and muleteers asking for tips at the end of a
journey. These practices are unapproved. In the interests of
goodwill it is recommended a tip is given of 2 or 3 cigarettes
or one small cigar after the work is completed; a good reason
for non-smokers to carry tobacco, also useful in many other
potential tipping situations. The Berbers use the word "cadeau"
when asking for a tip. They possibly know that formal tipping
is illegal in many public places in Morocco, and think that a
"present" is a suitable evasion.   The porter rate is not

absolutely fixed and can be calculated as half of the mule rate[']
per man; it normally only applies in the winter and early spring
when mules cannot be used in snow. The charge for guiding
services is subject to negotiation and a day rate of Dh. 40. 00
is the average at present.

Charges for coming downhill, or in the reverse direction,
are the same as uphill. At a high hut it is often possible to
agree a discount up to 20% with a muleteer arriving the same
day who has the prospect of returning "empty".

Specimen mule hire charges. One mule carries a load of
60 kg. = all baggage for a climbing party of two going uphill
with food and equipment (but not additional camping equipment)
for 4 to 5 days; or party of three for 3 days. Examples assume
that party carries nothing.

Imlil to: Sidi Chamharouch Dh. 10. 00 Lac d'Ifni 40. 00
      Neltner hut 30. 00 (loads are carried
      Tizi Oussem 20. 00 from the foot of the
      Lépiney hut 35. 00 Ouanoums col)
      Tacheddirt hut 20. 00 Tizi n'Tagharât 20. 00
          (porters only)

Tacheddirt to: Tizi n'Likemt 25. 00
      Tizi n'Tacheddirt 20. 00
      Oukaimeden, over Tizi n'Ouadi (n'Eddi) 30. 00

A loaded mule and its keeper goes uphill at 7-8 kph. The
muleman walks behind briskly or rides the animal according to
roughness and steepness of the trail. Even the fittest mountain-
eers will not be able to sustain this punishing rate of ascent
for more than an hour and there is no point trying. The muleteer halts about every 30 min. and waits dutifully for his cus-
tomers to catch up. The Berbers are totally reliable in this
matter. Whereupon the weakest member of the party (he has
already been spotted in the first 15 min.), but especially a
lady, is invited to mount the mule and ride for some distance,
or all the remaining distance if necessary (no extra charge!).
These halts are always made beside a large rock from which
the rider steps onto the mount. The walking action of an Atlas

mule, incredibly surefooted and inclined towards reluctance and laziness in its style, makes for a comfortable ride which does nothing for improving fitness and acclimatisation. Despite the speed of this ascent the muleteer rambling along behind his animal finds time to kick or push large stones off the trail, or to stop and talk to another native, or partake of a glass of mint tea being brewed by others along the wayside. The descent pace is much the same or rather slower - so that if you feel like a jogging finish of two, three and sometimes four hours following several days of fatigue on the big hot screes and endless rocks of the High Atlas, a Berber muleteer will just manage to keep ahead to the bottom. There however he will look as fresh as when he started and you may be feeling slightly the worse for wear.

<u>Aroumd</u>: this picturesque terraced village (1920m.) also goes under names spelt Aremd and Around; it appears higher up the Mizane valley, is built on the S (invisible) side of a broad stony spur above Imlil and is best reached by following the main mule trail on the R side to cross the river plain just beyond the village site (45 min.), see route to Neltner hut. An old CAF hut, no longer open, is one of the houses on the R side of trail as you reach the Aroumd plain. Accommodation in Berber houses, limited provisioning, at least one house rented by a trekking organisation for use of its holidaymakers. The population of Aroumd constantly pesters tourists and only a short visit is recommended. The Neltner hut trail proper bypasses the village.

<u>Imenane Valley</u>

A parallel valley to the Mizane, to its E, and bending due E in its upper reaches; from Asni by a long mule trail in 6 h. to Tacheddirt. The easiest and most direct approach to this village, a popular base centre, goes from Imlil E over the <u>Tizi n'Tamatert</u> (2279m.) by an excellent mule trail. Some years ago a jeep road was constructed to this pass on the Imlil side. Now the road is being extended to Tacheddirt and a gang is blasting a highway along the line of the mule trail. Jeeps and lorries ascending the Imlil side at present have to ford the Mizane river just above the village at a place which thankfully

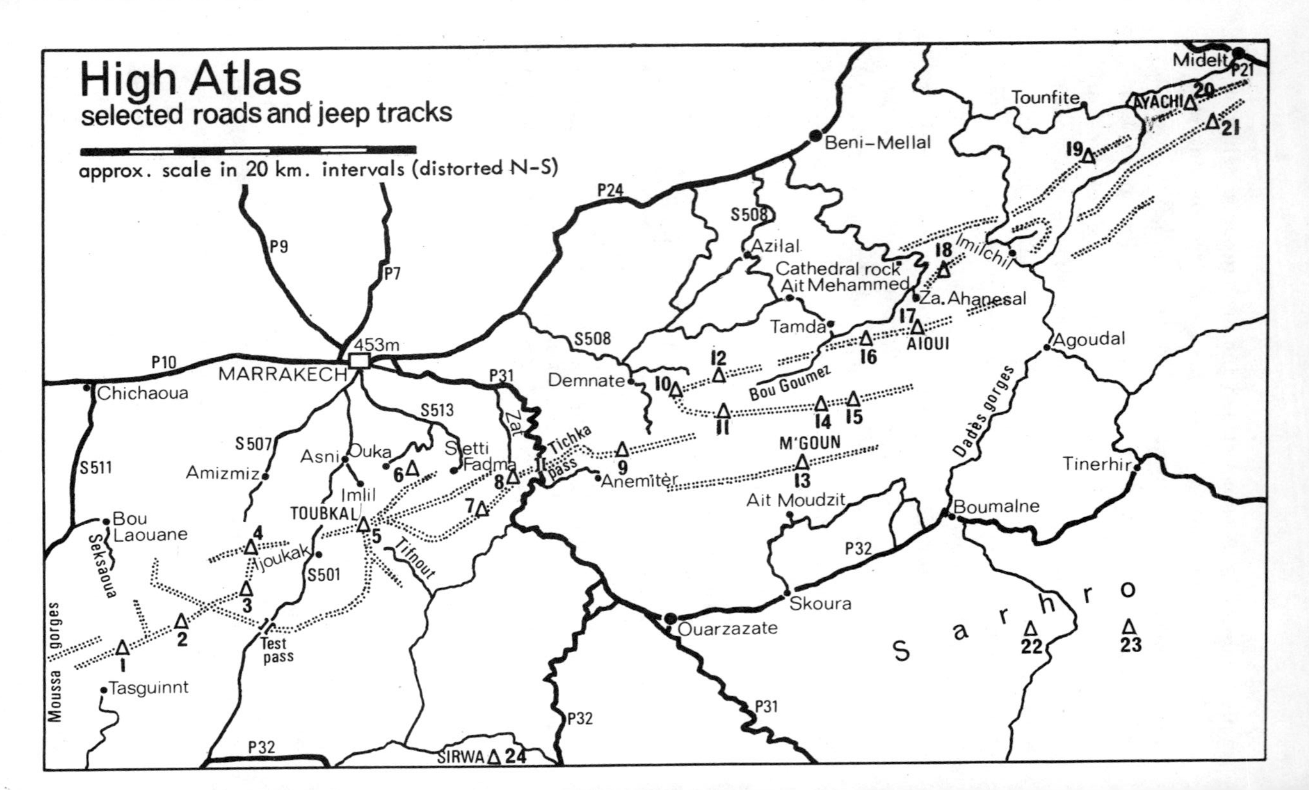

High Atlas
selected roads and jeep tracks
approx. scale in 20 km. intervals (distorted N-S)
Midelt
P21
Tounfite
AYACHI
20
21
19
Beni-Mellal
P24
P9
P7
S508
Azilal
Cathedral rock
Ait Mehammed
18
Imilchil
Za. Ahanesal
17
Tamda
AIOUI
16
Agoudal
S508
12
10
Demnate
Bou Goumez
14
15
11
MARRAKECH
453m
P10
Chichaoua
P31
S513
M'GOUN
13
Zat
Tichka pass
9
Anemiter
Ait Moudzit
S507
Asni
Ouka
Setti Fadma
6
8
Amizmiz
S511
Imlil
TOUBKAL
7
Tinerhir
Boumalne
Bou Laouane
Seksaoua
4
Ijoukak
5
Tifnout
S501
P32
3
2
Test pass
Skoura
Ouarzazate
S a r h r o
22
23
Moussa gorges
1
Tasguinnt
P32
P31
SIRWA
24

deters most motorists - but feasible from July onwards. On completion this road must attract the Berber transit bus and the quaint isolation of Tacheddirt will be lost forever.

Leave Imlil by the main unmade road and in a few min. reach a huge rock among trees on L. Descend under L side of rock, cross river by stepping stones and rejoin road. Fording place passes R of large rock. Now by road to first bend/ zigzags; leave it to go up a narrow lane between stone walls to a hamlet perched on a rock bluff. Go through middle of hamlet and in the same direction stay with original mule trail to reach road up to L. After a short distance quit road again and in the dry valley bed work up trail pleasantly to meet road coming from L nearly at top of pass ($1\frac{1}{2}$ h.). Vipers nest among the scrub in this top part.

---

1 Tinergouelt 3551m.
Aoulime 3482m.
2 Tichka 3351m.
Ras Moulay Ali 3349m.
3 Igdat 3616m.
4 Erdouz 3579m.
5 Toubkal 4167m.
6 Angour 3616m.
7 Taskkan'Z at 3912m.
8 Bou Ouriol 3578m.
9 Anrhomer 3607m.
10 Rhat 3781m.
11 Tignousti 3825m.
12 Ouriat 3050m.
13 M'Goun 4068m.
14 Tiferdine 3542m.
15 Ouaougoulzat 3770m.
16 Azurki 3690m.
17 Aioui 3382m.
18 Koucer 3093m.
19 Masker 3265m.
20 Ayachi 3747m.
21 Maoutfoud 3445m.
22 Fengour 2559m.
23 Mansour 2712m.
24 Sirwa (Siroua) 3305m.

A recommended diversion is to go up the steep scrub ridge opposite to the top of the Assaoun n'Tanamrout (2636m.), first to a shoulder which from below can be mistaken for the summit, then along a gradual ridge for some distance to the top (1¼ h.). Superb panorama of the Toubkal massif, quite the finest to be obtained in a day's walk from Imlil. Return to the col (45 min.).

On the other side the road traverses in and out of several broad ravines and round spurs, losing height all the way, narrowing into the original mule trail (at present) and contouring with gradual descent to grassy ground above the main stream in the Imenane valley. Descend parallel with a branch stream to reach the main one, cross it by stepping stones (Ouaneskra on 100m. map), and take mule trail on far side to a junction with trail coming up L side of valley from Asni. Continue up this R to reach the outskirts of Tacheddirt village (2314m.) (2 h., 3½ h. from Imlil. 2½-3 h. in reverse direction). Mule hire, see above.

<u>Tacheddirt</u>: small densely populated village, a hard working mountain community in the classic Berber mould. Field terraces come right up to the walled enclosure supporting the mule path along lower boundary of village, and these fields are seen in artistic patchwork along both sides of the valley. No shop or other facilities. Mule hire and local guiding services; bread and eggs can be purchased from households willing to sell. Camping is hardly feasible. CAF hut is first building seen on L above trail before entering village. Converted from a simplified stone fortification; terrace area with wall and outside water tap/trough, flanked one side by single storey block housing kitchen and separate toilet, the other side by a dormitory with tiny combined mezzanine sleeping area and area beside door for one table and two benches. Above this room and the terrace is another small blockhouse serving as a second dormitory. Total sleeping places for 15, single bunk beds with foam mattresses, no blankets or sheets. Small calor gas cooker and cooking utensils in kitchen.

Warden keeps doors locked but parties have generally been sighted long before they reach village and doors are open on arrival. Rough compared with Imlil but like all property with Berber caretakers looked after with loving care and kept immaculately clean. Rates as for Imlil. Bring all food from Imlil, or elsewhere. Your own stove is optional and depending on plans for moving on to other centres.

Main crossing from Tacheddirt to Oukaimeden by the Tizi n'Ouadi (n'Eddi) is described in reverse direction from latter centre (see below). Other passes out of the Imenane valley are described in the Mountain bases section.

OUKAIMEDEN

The highest base centre (2630m.) in the Toubkal region, primarily a ski resort with all services open from early December to end March or early April. At other times of the year, see below. Leaving Marrakech by the S513 a fast road across the plain comes up to the entrance of the Ourika valley. No garage on this road or in the narrower twisting section entering the valley and passing the opulent Ourika hotel to reach Aghbalou. Just before this village a prominent turning on the R (no. 6035A) is taken (43 km.). It proves to be a wider road and climbs steadily up the Lekak (Leqaq) valley with a few potholded sections to a number of zigzags, at the top of which note an unmade and unmarked forestry road coming in from the R (2351m.). Continue into a shallow valley near the main river, pass a small barrage and gatehouse to enter the large Oukaimeden plateau. Hotels and chalets all lie on the R side of the road, rising up the rocky hillside and connected by service lanes (29 km., 72 km. from Marrakech, bus service in winter and from early July to end September, 2 h.). Immediately after the first big hotel on R a parallel service road runs along the front of a group of three-storey chalet buildings. The white one at the inner end (unmarked) is the CAF hut.

Bus service from Marrakech to Aghbalou (usually spelt, Arhbalou), where taxi is available for continuing to Oukaimeden in the closed season; allowing for a scarcity of vehicles on the Oukaimeden road in closed season, easy hitch-hiking.

<u>Oukaimeden</u>: 4 large hotels, 3 smaller ones, pension chalets, apartments to rent, etc. Camping at an official site, services closed in early summer. Several small shops and hotel shops, restaurants and cafés. Telephones, postal service. Chairlift

to summit of Oukaimeden (3273m.), four skilifts and tows on surrounding nursery slopes. Except for two small shops with very limited provisioning and the permanently open CAF hut, all these facilities are closed down from early April to early July - the dead season but in fact the best time of year for mountain touring parties. No mule hire in this season but perfectly possible to come into Oukaimeden with mules from another centre. In this period all plans must revolve round the CAF hut. The Berber population has evacuated itself except for shepherds tending their animals on the lush pastures in summer and a few others with ongoing jobs at the resort. Free carparking in summer, charges made in winter season.

CAF Oukaimeden hut. The largest building of its kind in the Atlas and big even by Alpine standards. Warden and staff throughout year, normally only three in early summer. Roughly divided inside into two sections, each complicated in layout (corridors and confusing stairways), the building is of medium size hotel proportions with facilities to match. Total complement: comfortable sleeping places for at least 160. Electric light, huge kitchen with all modern conveniences and calor gas cooking range. Large wash rooms with a dozen hand basins in each, hot and cold running water; several flushing toilets and showers. Bar room, lounge rooms, games room, dining rooms; bandstand. In early summer you eat in the kitchen or its anteroom. At this time all cooking and cleaning up must be done by parties themselves; no meals can be bought or served by the staff; no food available on premises. Bring all food with you. Resident warden and wife are French and helpful to everyone. Overcrowding does not arise at this splendid establishment; quiet and restful in the "dead" season. Rates as for Imlil hut and no tips are solicited.

Two places of local interest at Oukaimeden are the prehistoric engravings and the panoramic Tizrag viewpoint. The first are mostly found along the inner side of a rocky rib immediately below but at a higher level than the barrage wall, this rib bounding one side of the road as it approaches the resort. Location diagram and key to symbols on noticeboard in hut hallway; 20 min. on foot. From road near gated entrance to plateau, for some reason pedestrians are barred from using the obvious walkway across top of dam, and should descend below wall to cross outflow stream on stones.

The road at upper end of resort reaches a junction with road to L (SE) running across plateau to chairlift carpark. By continuing straightahead it reaches at a bend the Tizrag col (2668m.), with a mule trail on the other side to Asni or Tacheddirt. Returning to the R it climbs to a television relay station looking like a space-age outpost, gated and private entrance. At last bend below this point, limited carparking on the verges. From here a track goes up over smooth rock slabs, to R then back L in 5-7 min. to the summit of the Ad. n'Tizrag escarpment (2740m.), marked by an orientation table on the edge of precipitous brown cliffs. By a direct ascent of slopes behind resort on foot, 25 min. Splendid views to N in Marrakech direction and more restricted panorama of main Toubkal region summits. Hemmed in below the Oukaimeden plateau is dominated on two flanks by the contrasting bulky shapes of Oukaimeden summit and the Angour (3616m.), the latter being the mountain par excellence hereabouts.

The following alternative scenic routes can be used to reach Oukaimeden from Marrakech or from Asni/Imlil. About 2 km. outside Tahannaout in the Marrakech direction is a cross country metalled road (no. 6034) of 20 km., joining the S501 and S513. Single lane, fairly fast, occasionally potholed. Take care at a confusing bend/junction near pt. 794m.

About 2 km. outside Tahannaout in the Asni direction is a signposted fork for Oukaimeden with a board translating as "Scenic forestry route". This is a splendid hair-raising journey, quite direct as an alternative approach from Marrakech, not recommended for cars larger than $1\frac{1}{2}$ litres. Follow the tarmac road which soon becomes a narrow dirt road with many zigzags and bends in the forested slopes on E side of the Fars valley. Depending on conditions, large holes and ruts need care in circumventing. The road climbs to the enclosing ridge crest, then a junction is reached in a large glade/saddle called Tassaft n'Tizi (1807m.), near the hamlet of Tadmamt and the better known holiday resort for Marrakech dwellers of Sidi Fars. Do not take road to these places. Turn sharp L (E) and drive for nearly one km. to a sharp fork R. Follow this road fork (no. 6040) in numerous zigzags with impressive glimpses of the Tizrag cliffs ahead. So the road works up to a forestry hut on the Tizi n'Taslitane (2200m.) by which the N end of the escarpment is turned along an exciting "corniche" which swings back S to join the regular Ourika-Oukaimeden road at pt. 2351m. (37 km. from Tahannaout) about $4\frac{1}{2}$ km. from the resort.

From Asni an unmade road (no. 6036) crosses the river then initially enters in the Imenane valley before climbing out of it to the E and passing the Iferhane (Ifghane) forestry hut reaches the hamlets of Sidi Fars and Tadmamt, where the previous route is joined; the most direct way by car from Imlil/Asni to Oukaimeden.

Oukaimeden to Tacheddirt

Over the <u>Tizi n'Ouadi</u> (n'Eddi), mule trail on both sides. Mule hire at Tacheddirt end only; for rates see Imlil subsection above.

From Oukaimeden follow road to chairlift carpark. Continue by unmade road, soon taking a L fork and staying with road until old shepherds' huts appear low down on slopes to L. Near this point the mule trail filters off R, working away from the road and valley bed and slanting across the mountainside above them. The trail leads without possible error to the col ($1\frac{3}{4}$ h., $1\frac{1}{4}$ h. in descent). 2928m.

Motorists can drive to carpark, saving 10-15 min. It is possible to drive rough road to junction with mule trail; a ford and some large stones may deter those with low-slung vehicles, otherwise easy and flat; saves 30 min. If you can drive this far you will be able to continue along lorry road in valley bed to site workings at the top - flat all the way; do not drive into workings and park at a convenient turning circle just outside them. From here go through workings on L side of stream and round a bend R into the narrows; cross to R of stream and ascend with poor track over easy ground not far from stream bed to join mule trail coming in from the R and higher up, almost at the col; saves 45 min.

On the other side of the col the trail divides immediately. The R-hand (direct) branch goes down a worn groove to numerous zigzags on steep scree slopes; it keeps to L side of the cwm, reaching scrub where a prominent branch goes R; keep L and cross a shoulder/col to enter a steep secondary valley. Look out for a pile of stones at the bottom of zigzags, marking point where this trail is quitted; the penalty for missing this turning is to join the mule trail near the bottom of the main Imenane valley with an annoying reascent along latter. At the proper turning, a little track traverses slightly downwards over scree and scrub to Tacheddirt, arriving exactly at the roof of the CAF hut ($1\frac{1}{4}$ h. in descent, $2\frac{1}{4}$ h. in ascent).

Without the obligation of plodding behind a muleteer, at the col it is better to take the L-hand track. This at first makes a slightly descending traverse for 5 min. to a little col, then descends steeply in a bouldery hollow in a line parallel to and some distance E of the main mule trail; a rapid descent leads across a shoulder into the steep secondary valley mentioned above, where the ways unite; some confusing shortcuts; 10 min. shorter altogether; doubtful merit in ascent in view of steepness.

OURIKA VALLEY AND SETTI FADMA

Probably the least frequented inroad to the Toubkal national park. It serves as the E end of the usual high level traverse of the region (although this is often continued to the Tichka road further E) and must be ranked as an important base for several outlying summits of considerable height.

From Marrakech, as for the regular route to Oukaimeden along the S513 road. This road continues narrow but good in the wooded defile of the Ourika valley to a roadhead and car-parking at the lower end of Setti Fadma village (1480m.), 67km. from Marrakech. Irregular bus service. At Asggaour hamlet, one km. before the roadhead, is the Auberge La Chaumière with Cat. 2 accommodation and a modest restaurant. The lower Ourika valley is dominated on its E side above Aghbalou village by Meltsene (3595m.) and the Yagour plateau (2726m.); the S side of the latter, above the Tizi n'Rhellis, has a series of prehistoric rock engravings more widespread than those seen at the Oukaimeden site.

<u>Setti Fadma</u>: one Berber inn and accommodation in houses; two or three small shops with reasonable provisioning, one with café and meals served on request. Camping possible with permission, not difficult to obtain. Mule and porter hire by private arrangement, rates not fixed. Considerable distances are involved for expeditions taken up the Ourika valley; its formidible length is well known to Atlas devotees. The CAF hut at Timichi hamlet (1850m.) is rarely used and will be found in a rough condition and without the customary appointments. This can be used as an overnight shelter by touring parties but is too low for most climbing expeditions. Determined mountain walking or climbing parties must be prepared to make a day's march from Setti Fadma to put up a high camp, or bivouac, before the main summits to the S and SW can be tackled. The mule trail from Oukaimeden to Setti Fadma over the Tizi n'ou Attar (formerly n'Ourhans) is described in the tours section of the guide.

Mountain Huts and other bases

<u>Ijoukak Hut</u>   1200m.

CAF supervised but not owned. Marked on map "Maison forestière", at top of little twisting side road to E of Test main
road, 300m. before the bridge at junction with Agoundis valley
(94 km. from Marrakech). Bus service. Inquire at inn near
bridge to ascertain that door is open, otherwise whereabouts
of key holder will be disclosed. 10 sleeping places, kitchen
area and utensils. Take your own stove. See comments about

Test pass road and alternative accommodation at beginning of previous section.

<u>Lépiney Hut</u>   3050m.

CAF.   After Jacques de Lépiney (d. 1942). Situated near top of the Azzaden valley whose upper half (called Aougdal n'Bou Idarene) lies roughly parallel with and to W of the Mizane. The lower half exits at Ouirgane (Wigane) on the Test pass road about 14 km. from Asni.
   Rarely visited and then usually by climbing parties. Much the best hut from which to ascend Tazaghârt by any route but increasingly ignored by mountain scramblers in favour of longer and more complicated ways from the cosmopolitan Neltner hut. Climbers will be attracted by the famous NE wall of Tazaghârt, the biggest and most impressive rockface in the area, and by specialised rock climbs on the W side of the Ouanoukrim-Tadat chain.   Again, the latter are much less frequented than corresponding routes on the E (Neltner) side.   Some climbers prefer to cross this chain by the Tadat col to reach the hut - shorter than the valley route but you run the risk of finding the door locked.
   For mule hire and porterage the Berbers at Imlil take loads down the Mizane and return over the Tizi n'Tacht to reach Tizi Oussem village. Or if short of time carry loads over the Tizi n'Mzic (2489m.) to Tizi Oussem for loading on mules. The latter is the walking route, and while classed as a mule trail is very steep on the W (Tizi Oussem) side. Beware of engaging mules, etc. at Imlil after 11.00 am. for a later start. Nothing will be said by the Berbers but you are unlikely to reach the hut before nightfall and will be persuaded to stop overnight (see below) and reach your destination the following morning with additional expense.
   Places for 20, foam mattresses, no blankets, limited cooking utensils, take your own stove and billycans. Warden lives at Tizi Oussem and door is locked when hut is unoccupied. Warden remains at hut when parties are in attendance but he does no cooking.

   From Imlil carpark leave village by rough road passing the stables. On R side at 200m. is a narrow unmarked gap between a rock and a stonewall.   Pass through this and follow a path between maize fields to a T junction with the more positive trail going L for Neltner hut.   Bear R along path ascending round a wooded shoulder above cultivated terraces to traverse W to the stream bed in the V-shaped valley below the Tizi n'Mzic.   On R side of stream go up through walnuts to cross
70

and recross the stream twice before finally rising on the R
side with an excellent mule trail to the col (2489m.), $2\frac{1}{4}$ h.

Just over the top the main trail goes straight down to Tizi
Oussem with an alternative at an easier gradient forking L.
Take the latter (SSW) until after crossing dry stream beds it
starts to descend more rapidly. A smaller track traverses
on a downward line ahead (SW) over steep stony ground to cross
a juniper shoulder followed by a further descent to a mule trail
coming up the valley from Tizi Oussem. This leads with a
reascent of 100m. to the Tamsoult huts (2300m.), $1\frac{1}{4}$ h. The
Moroccan Youth Sports Club owns a small hut here, Berber in
charge, which provides acceptable night-quarters for parties
arriving late. From here some parties reach the Lépiney hut
in under 2 h.; most will take a lot longer. Not advisable to
leave Tamsoult after 3.00 pm.

Above Tamsoult the path ascends the last cultivations to
cross the stream R below the entrance to a gorge forming the
main valley. (There is a direct way up this). It then works
steeply up the R side of a tributary valley for some distance
before returning L over a spur dividing it from the main one.
Here a grassy descent reaches the bed above the gorge and
follows up the L side, over a lateral spur and above the last
junipers, to cross a series of broad gullies filled with scrub
and thistles, with the angle moderating all the way. The hut
stands on a shoulder above the R (W) side of the stream $(3-3\frac{1}{2}$ h.,
$6\frac{1}{2}$-7 h. from Imlil).

<u>Neltner Hut</u>   3207m.

CAF. After Louis Neltner (b. 1904). Situated high up the Mizane valley and directly accessible from Imlil. More frequented
than all other huts and mountain bases put together because it
stands at the foot of Toubkal. Warden resident for long periods
at a stretch and door rarely locked.
A solid stone construction built in 1938, places for 29 in two
dormitories with foam mattresses, no blankets. Combined
living room and kitchen, calor gas cooking range and utensils.

A charge is made for use of same, also for hot water and cooking services provided by warden. Those with their own stoves, etc. are free to use them. Food normally not available; plentiful supply of soft drinks (Dh. 3.00 per bottle in 1979). Water in hut comes from a tank filled by warden from stream immediately below the outside toilet.

In spring mules carry to the snowline, thereafter porters must be used. The trail is normally clear for mules all the way from early May.

From Imlil leave the village as for the Lépiney hut (above). At the T junction bear L into an open wood where the trail is confused by stones and water trickles. At the top exit along a horizontal path beside a few houses and take numerous zigzags up a road-like section across rocky slopes to emerge at the Aroumd plain. Keep R till past the last house on R, then bear L across the broad stony plain, several tracks, to cross the main stream on the far side before the path is seen ascending slopes further up and L. Go up latter in zigzags to a level section running along to cross the stream R in the narrows just before Sidi Chamharouch (2310m.), $2\frac{1}{4}$ h. A diversion L of 3 min. leads to this hamlet which is raised among huge boulders; buffet - known to some as a robbers' den - and pastoral mosque with brilliant white roof. The main trail climbs directly above stepping stones in stream, zigzagging on a rocky slope and working L high above the valley bed. It eases off and continues in several fairly straight sections, gradually approaching the bed. The middle cwm is reached, from where the hut is seen, and this is crossed, always on the R side of the valley, passing eventually below the ruined site of the Isougane n'Ouagouns huts, and finally at a gentle angle over marshy ground to the hut standing above a fork in the stream ($2\frac{1}{2}$ h., $4\frac{3}{4}$ h. from Imlil).

Lac d'Ifni   2295m.

The only lake of any size in the Toubkal region. Its contours have changed with attempts to control the inflow for serving extensive irrigation and cultivations in the Tifnout valley below

72

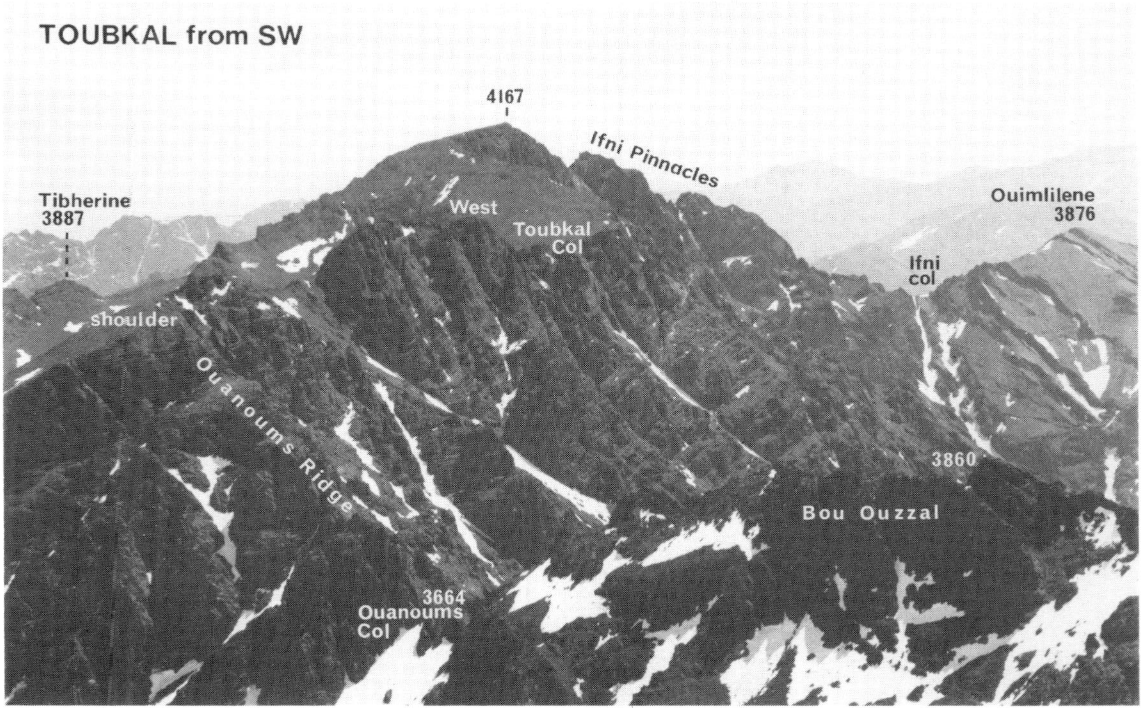

TOUBKAL from SW
4167
Ifni Pinnacles
Ouimlilene 3876
Tibherine 3887
West
Toubkal Col
Ifni col
shoulder
Ouanoums Ridge
3860
Bou Ouzzal
3664
Ouanoums Col

TOUBKAL WSW ridge
from Ouanoums col
pinnacle
normal start

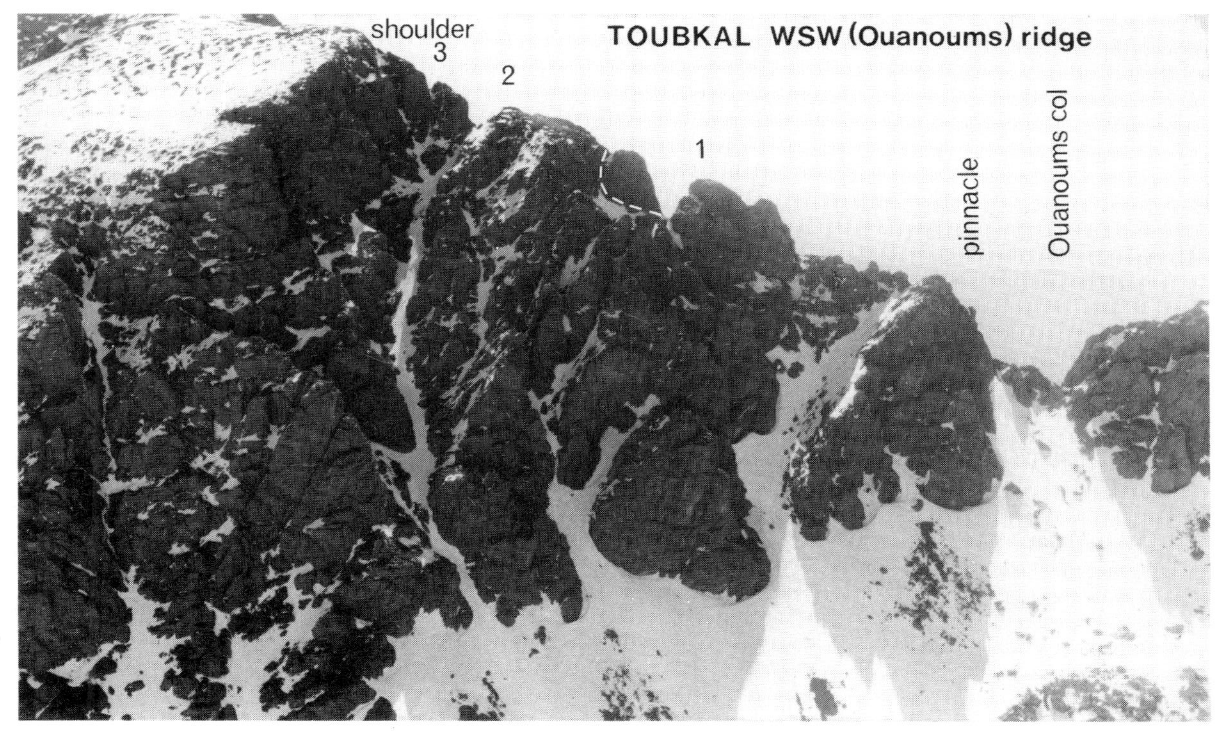

shoulder
3
2
1
TOUBKAL WSW (Ouanoums) ridge
pinnacle
Ouanoums col

Tizi n'Likemt
Azib col 3776
Anrhemer
TIGOURZATINE COL
Ad.nou Ahior
Tizi n'Likemt

Aksouâl
Azrou n'Tamadôt
AMGUERD N'OUKSOUAL
towers
Arhzane col
Tamda ravine

Bou Iguenouane
towers
3615
Tizi n'Likemt
Meqqoren cwm

TOUBKAL
Imousser
Tibherine
N cwm
S cwm

OUANOUKRIM
Ras
Akioud >
E ridge (roof)
Bou
Imrhas
col
NE couloir

Tadaft
Akioud
C N
NE ridge
NNW ridge
Amrharas
n'Iglioua
col

far you will be able to continue along lorry road in valley bed
to site workings at the top - flat all the way; do not drive into
workings and park at a convenient turning circle just outside
them. From here go through workings on L side of stream and
round a bend R into the narrows; cross to R of stream and
ascend with poor track over easy ground not far from stream
bed to join mule trail coming in from the R and higher up, almost at the col; saves 45 min.

On the other side of the col the trail divides immediately.
The R-hand (direct) branch goes down a worn groove to numerous zigzags on steep scree slopes; it keeps to L side of the
cwm, reaching scrub where a prominent branch goes R; keep
L and cross a shoulder/col to enter a steep secondary valley.
Look out for a pile of stones at the bottom of zigzags, marking
point where this trail is quitted; the penalty for missing this
turning is to join the mule trail near the bottom of the main
Imenane valley with an annoying reascent along latter. At the
proper turning, a little track traverses slightly downwards
over scree and scrub to Tacheddirt, arriving exactly at the
roof of the CAF hut (1¼ h. in descent, 2¼ h. in ascent).

Without the obligation of plodding behind a muleteer, at the
col it is better to take the L-hand track. This at first makes
a slightly descending traverse for 5 min. to a little col, then
descends steeply in a bouldery hollow in a line parallel to and
some distance E of the main mule trail; a rapid descent leads
across a shoulder into the steep secondary valley mentioned
above, where the ways unite; some confusing shortcuts; 10
min. shorter altogether; doubtful merit in ascent in view of
steepness.

OURIKA VALLEY AND SETTI FADMA

Probably the least frequented inroad to the Toubkal national
park. It serves as the E end of the usual high level traverse
of the region (although this is often continued to the Tichka road

---

- one
reach
by a
dit
b

oun
1400m
with Ber
side is mos.
The lake is
the S face of To
Pinnacles (SE) ridg
from the col to get at ь.
The southern high leve.
way, to continue by the 'ь.
Tacheddirt.

TIZI N'OUANOUMS   3664m.

Axe and possibly crampons useful to eь
Neltner hut traverse 50m. distance rather aь
traverse path to reach the original trail coming up
and bypassing the hut. Follow it, ignoring lesser branc.
In general keep slightly R, crossing the rough mountainsı
and later curving upwards and L well above the bed - snowfields
or large patches to end June. Latterly with a poor track and
a few cairns the trail attains a level plain in the bed; a few
large rocks and old moraines cut by small streams. Trend L
to a point directly under the obvious col up to L. Mules stop

here and porters carry loads as required. Go straight up the bad scree and rocks. Before July, long snow ribbons; before June a continuous snow slope may be found, making the work straightforward and pleasant. In bare conditions endeavour to follow the original zigzags and so reach the narrow saddle, a windy spot, $1\frac{3}{4}$ h. In descent, 1 h.

On the other side slither down a steep craggy ravine, easy but uncomfortable, with traces of a small track twisting back and forth, finally emerging at scree mounds, pt. 2841m. Always near the stream bed, an improving track in boulders follows one side or the other down to greener ground; keep along N edge of the lake, $2\frac{1}{2}$ h. In ascent, $4\frac{1}{2}$-5 h.

<u>Tifni-Tinzer basin</u>

A huge, complicated enclave and depression draining through several contributory valleys into the upper Ourika valley. The sub-ranges formed by Aksouâl, Iguenouane and Anrhemer enclose it on the N side; those of Tichki and Tinilim on the SW side; and the Ad. n'Dern and Iferouane on the S and E sides. The latter boundary, crowned by Iferouane, presents a challenge of distance and remoteness to the peak-bagger; the others are more accessible from slopes on the outer flanks of the basin.

The Tizi n'Tagharât gives access to the Tifni branch, the Tizi n'Ourai to the Tinzer (Tinzart) portion. Neither offers the most convenient way into the basin area. Despite the daunting riser, the easiest approach traverses the Tizi n'Likemt from Tacheddirt. Camping or sleeping in pastoral huts; bivouac material should be carried. Mules can enter and cross this area after end May. According to route and ultimate objective, the various groups of Berber huts in this great basin are so noted.

The gorges in the lower part of the Tifni outfall, under the walls of Anrhemer, are called "Kassaria" and empty into the upper Ourika valley; they afford a very steep and picturesque approach into the basin, not possible for mules, and normally taken by parties with porters from Setti Fadma. At least one porter should know the route well.

TIZI N'TAGHARÂT   3442m.

The big side valley E above Sidi Chamharouch (2310m.), reached from Imlil by the Neltner hut trail in $2\frac{1}{4}$ h. Reduced loads for mules; or porters. At the river crossing just below the hamlet pedestrians can take a small track on L side of the Mizane river and so avoid the hamlet. This rocky track ascends steeply in a curve L and after 30 min. crosses the tributary stream R to join the mule trail on this side. Mules approach from the hamlet by initially following the R side of the Mizane river to a suitable ford, and return L along a terraced trail into the side valley and on its R side. The trail is clear in endless stones and climbs with unremitting steepness and monotony in scores of zigzags, found in a neglected condition near the top, to the broad pass, 4 h. In descent, $2\frac{1}{4}$ h.

The trail divides. Ignore the R fork (SSE) which makes a high level up and down movement over the adjoining Agouni n'Isekdal col to the Tizi n'Terhaline (n'Ounar Imaghka) for a descent to the Tissaldai branch of the upper Tifnout valley. Make a gradual descent E straight ahead, across scree slopes to a shoulder called the Tizi Tifourhar (3315m.) from where a steeper descent in zigzags E leads to a gentle section. At this point the trail divides again. Descend R (S) to reach the Tifni huts (2820m.), situated on both sides of the Tifni stream bed ($1\frac{1}{4}$ h.); or continue by the traversing trail which soon turns SE to pass high above the Tifni huts on the N side of the valley. It can be followed to a shoulder on a prominent spur descending S from the Aksouâl massif. Here another track arrives from the Tifni huts below. By the same trail gradually approach the bed at its junction with the Tinzer valley, entering from the S where groups of huts are passed, shortly to reach the Likemt huts (2650m.) on the N side of the main stream. This site is the natural centre of the Tifni-Tinzer basin area, 3 h. from Tagharât col. In ascent, $5-5\frac{1}{2}$ h.

TIZI N'LIKEMT 3540m.

A large horizontal saddle, a famous Atlas mule trail, its screes having acquired notoriety among travellers. The saddle divides a long ridge capped by the Iguenouane and Aksouâl peaks, which can be reached by rather lengthy diversions from the col.

From Tacheddirt take the main mule trail up the valley. About 100m. past the last houses the trail divides; zigzags L mark the way to the Tacheddirt col. Keep ahead along the horizontal part to ford the river and return R on the opposite bank along a stonewall enclosure. Follow the obvious trail across the bottom of a side valley, waterfalls during spring in its stream higher up, to the next opening, more arid looking. Turn up this near the bed where the trail keeps L and eventually enters a large hollow halfway up to the skyline. The trail twists R then L among large blocks, snow patches to late spring, and rises to long scree slopes ascended by interminable zags, relenting slightly as the col is attained, $3\frac{1}{2}$-4 h. In descent, $2\frac{1}{2}$ h.

On the other side descend pleasantly at first bearing R along a good track which lower down keeps to the R side of the steeper valley gorge dropping directly to the Likemt huts (2650m.), 2 h. In ascent, 3 h.

The highest huts and shelter for parties intent on climbing the Iferouane are found on the mule trail leading from the Tinzer gorge to the Tizi n'Ourai. To reach these from the Likemt huts descend the main valley to below the last huts, then cross the river (ford) R and ascend the opposite side to a level shoulder in a spur dividing the main valley from a subsidiary gorge to the E. The trail contours SE in and out of gullies above this gorge and soon crosses it to make a short ascent to the huts known as Tinissane (about 2720m.), $1\frac{1}{2}$ h. from Likemt huts.

At all these native hut sites water might be scarce after mid August.

<u>Tizi n'Tacheddirt</u>   3172m.

This pass, leading from the Imenane valley (Tacheddirt

village) to the upper Ourika valley, can be used as a mountain base for several important excursions, thereby cutting out the repetitive and tedious ascent and descent from and to Tacheddirt. The Ourika side is very long and described in the touring section of the guide. The top is a broad and partly grassy plateau without water in summer and generally too exposed to wind for comfortable camping or a bivouac. At the lower E edge of this (Ourika side), some 400m. distant and 70m. lower, is a group of rocks in a little hollow near the trail, affording good shelter. Berbers have erected windbreaks and shepherds often use it. Water available to late April; after that parties must carry water from Tacheddirt. Mule hire easy and convenient, and the whole trip from Imlil-Tacheddirt to col is easily accomplished in a day.

From Tacheddirt start as for the Likemt col; after the last houses take the L fork in a few zigzags to continue up the L side of the Imenane valley; the col at the top is visible all the way. Avoid sundry branches L in the lower part, up to a level section running into a rib on the R. From this point the original mule trail is confused by many shortcuts; the latter tend to keep R (but still on L side of main stream bed) while the proper route commences a series of zigzags up to the L; they come to within 150m. of the rocks forming the huge S face of Angour before returning to join the various lines of shortcuts. The upper section is much longer than it looks and the easy angled mule trail works some distance R before slanting back to the frontal approach not far from the col, $2\frac{1}{2}$ h. In descent, $1\frac{3}{4}$ h.

NOTES ON TRAINING WALKS

Imlil: The Assaoun n'Tanamrout is the best excursion, also the shortest; described under Imenane valley in the Valley Bases section. Its pendant on the other side of the valley is the Tasghimout (2664m.), reached from the Tizi n'Mzic on the Lépiney hut trail up a moderately steep scrub crest in 30 min., about $2\frac{3}{4}$ h. from Imlil. More ambitious, on the other flank of the col rises the impressive Ad. Adj or El Hadj (3129m.). The ridge from the col is continuously steep and later rocky, and should be turned on the R side more in the summit line. This ridge joins the NE ridge at an easy angle near the top. A superb viewpoint, $2\frac{1}{4}$ h. from Mzic col, $4\frac{1}{2}$ h. from Imlil.

Tacheddirt: Worthwhile walks are absent if the ascent to high passes is ruled out. Angour is too long to be classed as a training peak, and the Oukaimeden summit is a fastidious excursion from this centre.

Oukaimeden: Its namesake peak is an obvious objective described in the next section of the guide.

Lépiney hut: Anyone going to this mountain base should already be fit and will not need to indulge in training climbs proper. Relatively low altitude ascents from this hut are generally rock climbs.

Neltner hut: Conversely, more than half the parties tramping to this hut have come straight into the area from the plains, or worse still off an aeroplane from distant places, and are shattered from the outset by the walk up the Mizane valley. The Ouanoums and Ouagane passes are at a sensible distance from the hut, even though the same ground may be covered again in longer expeditions. Rock climbers aim for Tadat in spite of its steep, tiring approach. The least fatiguing four-thousander is the Ras n'Ouanoukrim. All are described in the next section.

Toubkal Region main summits

To avoid over numerous cross references descriptions are not presented in strict topographical order but eventually read from W to E along the main watershed.

Grading of routes is not normally given for ordinary ascents unless they present special problems. An indication of the terrain encountered and the effort required is considered sufficient for walking and scrambling. For notes given on mountaineering routes proper, technical climbing grades have been revised in accordance with modern estimates. Many of the early routes in the massif were over-graded, the term "difficile" being used frequently for pitches of II+/III-. Similarly many post World War 2 routes have been overrated by enthusiasts (some put at TD+) and are cut down accordingly. For simplicity, the UIAA scale in roman numerals applies; their adjectival equivalents for the overall impression of a route are ignored.

JBEL TOUBKAL   4167m.

Celebrated as the highest mountain in North Africa, it has made no reputation in mountaineering circles and has proved more attractive to a broad spectrum of humanity that climbs mountains for recreation. Most of its flanks are composed of shifting scree slopes; it has fine cliffs in one part of the S quarter; the ridges are always more interesting and two are fine rock climbs of no special difficulty. The rock is generally insecure, improving on the ridges but sufficiently variable to exercise caution everywhere. Winter ascents are common but take longer due to mixed snow conditions and possibly weather. Springtime ascents are the most enjoyable when much of the abominable scree might be found covered with hard snow; then the ground can be climbed quickly in crampons. Also at this time the ridges should be found free from snow and verglas, imparting conditions comparable with the Alps in summer.

The summit area is a gently inclined plateau of stones, roughly triangular shaped, and in poor visability care is needed to steer a correct descent course. A strong, bitterly cold wind blows across the summit on average every three or four days in spring and summer; it might relent in the autumn. This is a fair weather sign, the prevailing currents coming from the S, which often manifest broken cloud cover after mid-day. A N wind means unsettled weather although it may run in this direction during the afternoon and evening, either as a local phenomenon in the high valleys or as a general meteorological condition lasting several hours. To comprehend weather patterns in this part of the High Atlas, visitors with good experience of wind and weather omens in the Alps have to reverse by 180° the customary directional indicators. The summit wind can be as chilling as an Alpine storm, lowering the temperature well below freezing for which the only protection is good mountain clothing.

In common with other great continental peaks the summit views are something less than perfect because all the ground near and far lies below and tends to look flat. The most tantalising prospect from Toubkal, haze permitting, opens in the southern direction to reveal the layered distances of the Sahara plateaux broken at one point like an upturned basin by the extinct volcano Siroua (Sirwa).

At present climbed by some 500 persons each year. First European ascent: V. Berger, H. Dolbeau, Marquis de Segonzac, 12 June, 1923. By a British party: B. Beetham, G. Thomson, April, 1927.

<u>Normal Route by South Cwm</u>. Irhzer n'Ikhibi South. The western flank of Toubkal, rising above the Mizane valley, is deeply gouged by two cwms designated N and S, which are divided by the WNW ridge coming down from the summit area. The Neltner hut stands below the entrance to the S cwm. In late summer a vague track with misleading variations can be followed all the way to the top. In late spring snow cover may extend from the hut to the top of the cwm headwall, still leaving the worst scree to be ascended laboriously. For those not in training or without preparation considerable effort may be involved; otherwise easy and hands are nowhere needed.

Behind the hut descend to cross the stream gorge and make a rising traverse L over grass and rocks forming a steepening

80

in the Mizane bed to attain a boulderfield higher up, 15 min.
Turn towards the mountainside and scramble a loose scree
slope for 75m., then traverse up L to reach the top of a rockband closing the base of the S cwm. Move L then ascend the
cwm bed, bearing slightly L then R, eventually keeping close
to the ridge flank on L, passing large blocks in a gutter and
always near the bed, so rising into a little rock plain. Cross
this to another short riser, keeping slightly R and so reach
the foot of the headwall in a stony hollow. Go up somewhat L
of the obvious exit to the lower edge of a huge inclined screefield running up to the Tizi n'Toubkal (3940m.) on the skyline.
At the top of the headwall keep L along a promising track; it
bears L up a scree slope, away from the still distant col;
these are the screes for which Toubkal is remembered. Towards the L side of this area a track goes straight up reaching
an angle of 35° where three steps are taken to gain one; clearly
better for descent. Keep somewhat R and zigzag up loose
ground to a little gap in the ridge coming up from the col;
sudden view across a deep ravine in S face cliffs to summit
above. Traverse horizontally below L side of rising crest to
reach the abovementioned direct track arriving from below.
Continue this traversing movement below the crest on the hut
side, a long crescent R and so exit on the summit plateau which
leads by keeping slightly L above the S face cliffs to an enclosure and cairns, 4 h. In descent, 2 h.

<u>North Cwm</u>. Irhzer n'Ikhibi North. See above. This cwm is
more solid underfoot but holds less snow than the S one. You
start badly by making a descent to enter it, then quicker terrain
enables time to be gained. The N and S cwms are frequently
combined to make a simple traverse of the mountain. Recommended.

Descend the valley trail for 5 min. then cross the river R
on grass and follow this bank. Ahead and above on your flank

lies the opening to the N cwm, defended by a huge moraine.
Make a rising traverse above some isolated blocks near the
stream and find a small track slanting up the loose moraine to
reach its crest. Follow crest to a large bouldery crescent
above the R side of the bed. Work along this and at the far end
go into the bed where the angle relaxes. Now go up in the
bottom round a corner to steeper ground which is cut by several
rockbands. Climb through these easily or turn them L, with
much unpleasant scree, finally mounting a steep opening L in
the headwall to an exit R over scree. Before mid May a lot of
this terrain will be snow covered. Join an obvious col in the
main ridge above. A track keeps slightly L up the fairly rocky
NE ridge of the mountain and rises regularly for 150m. to the
summit plateau, $4\frac{1}{2}$ h. In descent, $2\frac{1}{2}$ h.

Popular additions for a party coming down this cwm are -

Imousser 4010m.

From col at foot of the NE ridge of Toubkal ascend a short
ridge opposite to a forepeak in 15 min. Abseil 6m. to a gap
below and ascend an exposed continuation rib to summit. The
gap and rib are avoidable by a big detour and circular movement on L side. Reascent from gap, III.

Tibherine 3887m.

From the exit scree slope just below col at foot of NE ridge of
Toubkal, traverse more or less horizontally under rocks of
the Imousser to reach a gap between the latter and Tibherine.
Take the ridge above by an easy scramble to summit which is
strewn with aircraft wreckage, 30 min.

West-South-West (Ouanoums) Ridge.

By Alpine standards quite
a good rock climb on mostly sound granite; loose material
everywhere needs care; often verglassed in winter. One of
the most popular routes of its standard in the area and the most
accessible sporting way up Toubkal. III-, with an avoidable

pitch of IV.   The ridge rises in four steps, the first three
having quite prominent features and sub-divisions.   200m.
from col to the Ouanoums shoulder; after that scrambling and
scree.   First reported ascent: B. Beetham, P. Brogden,
August, 1930.

From the Tizi n'Ouanoums (q. v. $1\frac{3}{4}$ h. from Neltner hut)
ascend R side of crest on scree to a wall; climb this on R side
(II+) for two pitches to ledges below a large finger pinnacle.
Continue by chimney (III-) on R side of pinnacle to gap, then
two pitches along the nice crest, over a sharp hump and turning
a crooked gendarme on the R (II+). From a ridge saddle climb
a facet by a chimney system with short movements R (III-) for
three pitches and at the top cross platforms to a short step
taken direct (II) to the first scree head. Now descend to a gap
40m. below, with an awkward bulging crack (III), convenient
for an abseil.   The next step presents a 40m. wall. Either
climb this direct by a fine crack (IV), or turn it by traversing
L (hut side) to a scree/snow terrace then reascending a loose
gully to exit L above the wall by broken rocks to a large scrée
head.   Follow the dipping crest to a wall forming L side of
ridge.   Climb this direct and keeping slightly R using an obvious chimney line for two pitches (II+) to a rock head. Descend to a slight gap and finish up a short crest on good holds
at the Ouanoums shoulder (3850m.), $2\frac{1}{2}$-$3\frac{1}{2}$ h. from col.

Rubble and scree over two rock knobs into a little saddle is
followed by a sharp, steep ridge ascended at grade I by keeping
just L of crest.   This finishes on scree forming the roof of
Toubkal West (4020m.), 30 min. Descend rocks and scree to
the Tizi n'Toubkal (3940m.) and ascend the continuation ridge
on bad scree, keeping L below crest to where the normal S
Cwm route is joined and followed to the top, 1 h., about $6\frac{1}{2}$ h.
from Neltner hut without halts.

South-East (Ifni Pinnacles) Ridge.   An impressive staircase

rising from the Col d'Ifni (3750m.). Rarely climbed because
the approach from the Tizi n'Ouanoums is long and fatiguing;
a complicated but technically easy traverse of 3 h. or more
under the S face cliffs and ravines of Toubkal. Col d'Ifni is
finally reached by a narrow scree gully, snow until May. The
ridge goes up in two big steps to the Aig. d'Ifni (4080m.); by
the crest direct IV, or by turning movements on R side, II+.
After a saddle the summit plateau is reached by climbing a
chimney and slabs (III+) giving on to easy ground, 3-4 h. from
Col d'Ifni. First ascent: J. de Lépiney, A. Stofer, 12 September, 1927.

Along the traverse from the Ouanoums col to the Ifni col
rises the very steep but essentially broken S wall of Toubkal.
Continuous climbs of 400m. have been made here, at least
grade III+.

AFEKHOI   3755m.

After the Imousser the main ridge running NE from Toubkal
crosses a nodule, the Little Imousser, dips to the Tizi n'Imousser (3650m.), then rises shortly to Afekhoi (various spellings) which like the Imousser is often mistaken for Toubkal by
parties coming up to the Neltner hut. Not worth climbing for
itself, and traversed by the few parties that undertake to follow
this entire ridge over Tichki to the Tagharât pass.

TICHKI   3753m.

After Afekhoi the main ridge falls to the Tizi n'Tichki (3540m.)
and continues with small gaps and knobs all much the same
height (Agoujdad n'Tichki, 3607m.) to a group of squat towers,
the main obstacle on this ridge (avoidable by tortuous turning
movements) before mounting to the broad summit of Tichki,
overlooking the Tagharât pass at a complicated junction of
shattered ridges.
Above this pass the N ridge gives friable scrambling near
the top but no difficulty, $1\frac{1}{2}$ h., about $5\frac{1}{2}$ h. from Sidi Chamharouch. The easiest walking route from the Tagharât pass
(q.v.) takes the R (SSE) trail towards the Agouni n'Isekdal
saddle (3650m.); in the large shallow hollow before this bear
R to ascend a bleak stony cwm SW at a moderate angle to reach
the E ridge of the mountain which is followed briefly on its R

side to summit, $1\frac{3}{4}$ h. from Tagharât pass.

TOUBKAL WEST   4020m.

The great scree mound seen to the R of the Tizi n'Toubkal from
the headwall of the S Cwm route (q. v. above). From col, 20
min. Crossed by parties coming up the WSW ridge (above). A
number of technical rock climbs have been made on its spurs
and buttresses above the Neltner hut in grades III and IV.

OUIMLILENE (DÔME D'IFNI)   3876m.

Curiously stratified promontory rising from the outward end
of the Col d'Ifni, the latter being used for access to the SE
ridge of Toubkal (above).   No interest, easily attained by a
knobbly crest and scree from this col.

BOU OUZZAL (UZZAL)   3860m.

Granite roof with four summits numbered from the S end, the
first being highest, between the Ouagane and Ouanoums cols.
The ridge traverse is grade II with variations, or III direct.
A good training exercise for rock climbers. Short routes on
W side buttresses up to grade V+, reached in $1\frac{1}{2}$ h. from Nelt-
ner hut.

OUANOUKRIM   4088m.

The second highest mountain in the region and about the second
most popular.   Easier and less effort required than Toubkal.
It forms two summits, N (Ras, 4083m.) and S (Timesguida,
4088m.), divided by a broad scree/snow saddle. The Ras top
is seen from the neighbourhood of the Neltner hut at the back
of the Mizane valley.   Excellent views of the Toubkal chain
and south across the Sahara. Less satisfactory outlook along
the Ouanoukrim chain to N and a rather dull view of the rear-
ward side of the Tazaghârt plateau. Probably not climbed by
a European party before 1924.

<u>Normal Route from Tizi n'Ouagane by East Ridge.</u> The upper
screes covering the roof of the E ridge fortunately lie at a
moderate angle; this slope clears quickly of snow but continuous snow can be found in the Mizane bed right up to the col
as late as June; otherwise a mule trail in a bad state of repair.

Normally not possible to cross this pass with a mule before
mid July; the other (S) side is steeper and the snow lies there
just as long.

From the Neltner hut follow trail up valley as for the Tizi
n'Ouanoums (q. v.) to the level plain bed. Continue in the bed,
through narrows then up broad slopes cut by large rock islands.
Turn these on the L along the slope below the Bou Ouzzal. In
dry conditions many zigzags in scree and rocks on the R flank
lead to the col (3735m.). With frozen snow the angle rarely
exceeds 20° and the slopes can be mounted, axe in hand, without
crampons (2 h.).

From the col climb the broad ridge on broken rock keeping
R, bits of track, to a nick behind a trident gendarme. Go
straight up crest on good rock to a step. Move R and traverse
into a short gully which is climbed with a side rib back to ridge.
Follow ridge and soon move to R side to finish on a scree head.
Snow or scree straight ahead lead on to the large roof on L side
of ridge. In general keep 30m. distance from crest and plod
up to join crest at the apparent summit which is a forepeak.
Descend W and reascend across a small gap to reach the top
of Ras, $1\frac{1}{4}$-$1\frac{1}{2}$ h. , $3\frac{1}{2}$ h. from Neltner hut. In descent, 2 h.

To continue to the slightly higher S summit in full view, descend into gap and traverse horizontally below forepeak to a
rocky slope leading down to broad saddle of scree or snow.
Ascend the other side keeping somewhat R to a broad ridge
hump and move L along it to cairn, 15-20 min. from Ras.

In descent a shortcut can be taken from saddle, by making a
descending traverse over scree roof to join the E ridge near
its scree head at base of roof.

Ras North-West Ridge (from Tizi n'Bou Imrhaz). Not a particularly interesting ascent, better done in spring when snow
can be found to the col; otherwise rough terrain. The ridge
is quite steep and grade I.

After the narrows in the approach to the Tizi n'Ouagane as for the normal route, turn R into a side valley mounting below rocks of the Ras E ridge, following a rising terrace along L side of lower gully then crumbling slopes in the bed to a head-wall of loose rock and the Tizi n'Bou Imrhaz (3875m.), marked by a rock thumb on its R side, $2\frac{1}{2}$ h. Turn L up the ridge, narrow at first then broader and steeper with some friable rock to arrive suddenly on top of Ras, 1 h., $3\frac{1}{2}$ h. from Neltner hut.

<u>Ras North-East Couloir</u>. This gully drops from the gap between forepeak and summit, as crossed by the normal route. 250m. at an angle of 35° down to the Irhzer n'Bou Imrhaz lateral valley (see above). Nasty scree in summer but affords an excellent training climb on snow in spring; recommended for ascent or descent by competent parties, I+. With crampons and good conditions, the quickest way up or down the mountain, $3\frac{1}{4}$ h. from Neltner hut.

<u>North Face</u>. Between the two abovementioned routes. Climbs of 250m., IV.

OUANOUKRIM CHAIN - GENERAL

The rock ridge running N from Ouanoukrim to Aguelzim en-closes the W side of the Mizane valley, and beyond to Imlil. It is the most frequented sub-chain in the region, having some resemblance in ridge forms and salient buttresses to more familiar Alpine granite ridges. Several comparisons have been made but all fail when quality and continuous length be-come the yardsticks. Some individual modern routes, though short, are outstanding but the enduring feature of the chain remains its main ridge traverse and a small collection of pin-nacled subsidiary spurs giving rock climbs mostly in grades III and IV.

The W side of the chain is not immediately flanked as might be expected by the Azzaden valley whose upper section is called the Aougdal n'Bou Idarene where the Lépiney hut is situated. Behind the Tamsoult huts at the bottom of the Idarene gorge an intermediate hanging valley called Timellilt (Timlit) pene-trates in a parallel direction, roughly S, to peter out under

the N facet of Biguinoussene and the adjoining Tadat col. Therefore only the higher S part of the chain after Biguinoussene is
directly accessible from the Lépiney hut.

AKIOUD   4010m.

The first significant summit N of Ouanoukrim. After the Tizi
n'Bou Imrhaz four towers rise on the ridge, the second designated Akioud S (3960m.), the third Akioud Central (3970m.),
the fourth Akioud N (4010m.). The deep gap beyond the N
summit is the Tizi n'Amrharas n'Iglioua (3815m.).
    Akioud S has a grade V/V+ route of 200m. among others on
its E face (fine crack to L), reached from the Bou Imrhaz side;
Akioud N has a classic and exposed grade IV among others on
its NE face, reached from the Iglioua side. The main SE ridge
over or round its tower summits is II/III according to route
taken. The normal route takes the main NNW ridge.

North-North-West Ridge. A blunt, broken spur above the Tizi
n'Amrharas n'Iglioua. This col (3815m.) is the easiest and
most frequented crossing point in the chain. It is too far N to
connect directly with the highest cwm (Arhzane) of the Azzaden
valley and the Lépiney hut, but the latter can be reached by a
rough traverse to the adjoining Melloul col. Parties are recommended to go up and down the NNW ridge of Akioud N as an
extra summit on the way to or coming back from a day on
Tazaghârt.

From the Neltner hut follow the valley trail as for the Tizi
n'Ouanoums (q. v.). On reaching the level plain in bed and
before a point below the latter col work R into a deep U-shaped
valley running up and bending slightly L to the Ouanoukrim
chain ridge. Pleasant all the way up on frozen snow; keep L
in the lower part then make a fairly steep rising traverse R in
the upper, crampons useful, to the ridge gap on the R (N) side
of a dividing rock knob. In late season, some bad scree and
traces of a track, $2\frac{1}{2}$ h. In ascent from this side it is quicker
to strike up the last scree slopes and reach the ridge above
the col near the foot of a step. Now continue round the W side
on broken rock and ascend above the step to continue on the

OUANOUKRIM chain
Section of east side
A
B
D
E
F
G
H
J
A Clochetons
B Tower
D Biguinoussene
E Tadat
F Tadat col
G Nameless top, c.3820m.
H Approach from Neltner hut to Tadat ravine
J Biguinoussene ENE ridge

TADAT
N side

Bou Iguenouane (left) and Adrar nou Ahior seen along ridge from the Tigourzatine col.

B Grouden col
C Gap with I⊢ chimney
D Upper double step
E Central couloir
F East(ern) couloir
G Western groove
H Far left gully
J Gendarmes ridge
K 150m. chimney buttress

L Triple buttress
M White ridge
N Main north summit
O Oukaimeden 3273m.
P West ridge access point from Grouden col
S South summit
T Tissi plateau
TC Tacheddirt col
TR Tissi ravine

NGOUR South face

ANGOUR
from Ouadi col
N
3616
S
W ridge
Itbir col

A Itbir col

B Grouden col

C Gap with I+ chimney

CL Chairlift station

D upper double step

N North buttress

O Oukaimeden plateau

P West ridge access point from Grouden col

A East top (3892m.)
B Central top
D West top (3885m.)
E Tigourzatine col
F NE ridge quit point
N N face
T Tissi plateau, Angour
TC Tacheddirt col below,
   spur to Tigourzatine
   col rising right

broad spur to a narrowing which remains easy to the N peak,
45 min., 3¼ h. from Neltner hut.

TADAFT   c. 3900m.

An imposing rock tower dominating a side ridge extending NE
from Akioud Central peak; the gap between the two is called
the Amguird n'Bou Imrhaz (c. 3850m.). The base on all sides
is lapped by scree slopes. The easiest way up, a traverse
over the main NE ridge and descent by abseils to the gap,
whence Akioud is reached, is one of the best rock climbs of
its standard in the Toubkal region, IV-/IV, 300m. C. Beau-
rieux, J. Dresch, J. de Lépiney, 29 June, 1935. The N face
of the tower (Iglioua side) has several routes of V, 100m.,
while there is similar but easier climbing on the S face.

AFELLA   4015m.

One of the most visited summits of the Ouanoukrim chain. The
prow (S end) overlooking the Iglioua col (see above) is now
measured as 4015m. (demoted from 4043m.); while the N end
was formerly put at 4040m., no height is shown on the latest
map; the steadiest hand clinometer reading that can be taken
between the two indicates that the N end of this saddle summit
must be a little higher.
   Of great topographical importance, the connecting ridge and
neck of the Tizi Melloul (3860m.) is formed on the W side of
this saddle summit, forging the link between it and the great
Tazaghârt plateau.
   The mountain has one practical route for experienced walkers
with a more direct variation for climbers. The approach
passes below the SE face of 500m., cut by a central couloir
which offers the finest grade V route to be done from the Neltner hut. Other long technical routes here.

West Flank Normal Route. A circuitous way of reaching the
top, turning the broad prow facing SSE above the Tizi n'Amrharas n'Iglioua. The same approach is used by parties bound
for Tazaghârt. Parties starting from the Lépiney hut come up
to the Melloul col (q. v.) to join the same finish (4 h.).

As for the NNW ridge of Akioud N (above), to the col, 2½ h.
Traverse down and round to L, working over broken rock and
screefields to turn N in a slightly rising movement with the
Tizi Melloul ahead. Join the broad spur rising from this col

to the summit saddle about halfway up, then take the spur, on snow to June, to the top, $1\frac{1}{4}$ h., $3\frac{3}{4}$ h. from Neltner hut.

Rock climbers can go up the prow by a meandering route following a system of steep screebands and rockbands cut by gullies, first trending L, then direct, and finally R, turning pt. 4015m. on R side. II/II+, but mostly loose rubble.

CLOCHETONS 3930m.

Beyond Afella the main ridge northwards is nicely serrated to Biguinoussene. Halfway along and just before the lowest ridge gap rises a cluster of spires, a double central tower and more isolated prongs to N and S. While these have an overall height of 70m., in the ridge line they rise some 15m. Much emphasis used to be placed on the difficulty of this obstacle for ridge traversers; in reality there are three short pitches of II/II+. Climbed from the Neltner hut as a training exercise, particularly in spring or earlier when the approach up the Irhzer Ikhelloun can be made on frozen snow. The bottom of this steep couloir/ravine lies 10 min. away from the hut door. Mid season or later the bed is terrible scree and is only advised as a means of descent. At the top exit L to join ridge and return R over the Clochetons.

BIGUINOUSSENE 3990m.

An attractive rock peak nearly always climbed after a visit to Tadat. The S ridge is part of the Ouanoukrim chain traverse. The NNE ridge is the normal route, from the Tadat col. The long, very broken and discontinuous ENE ridge seems to be rarely tried; poor rock, II+. On the Azzaden/Lépiney hut (W) side the NW ridge and N face give excellent rock climbs, IV and V.

<u>North-North-East Ridge.</u> From the scree saddle adjoining Tadat (see below) ascend the broad broken crest line, keeping R to avoid short steps, and so reach the top in 45 min., $3\frac{1}{4}$ h. from Neltner hut.

TADAT 3760m.

A much courted rock finger standing 30m. high in the long saddle N of Biguinoussene. An essential and traditional objective for rock climbers staying at the Neltner hut.   The approach, an alleged "mule trail", is quite exhausting and does not represent the ideal "training walk" claimed for it. Most of the trail has disappeared and cannot be seen or found with snow cover which is common to end May or later. Care needed in descent on soft snow. The height of this tower was originally grossly overestimated, and speculators reducing it to c. 3650m. have been misled by equally wrong spot heights along the ridge to Aguelzim; the flattish summit to the immediate N (nameless, c. 3820m.) is not that of Aguelzim which is found 2 km. further N.

From the Neltner hut the approach to the Tadat col is put at grade I/I+ owing to the nature of the ground and its continuous steepness. Facing the hut door take a good traverse path across two snow tongues (to mid season) to where it appears to mount L and become faint, 10 min. Continue R on scree and broken rock and get on to a screeband/terrace running R at a higher level. Cross this horizontally then ascend to a shoulder, in fact a point low down on the ENE ridge of Biguin-oussene, another 15 min. Traverse horizontally into the big gully beyond, the Tadat ravine. In good snow conditions crampons are essential for steady progress. Climb it direct for 150m. at about 35° to below a noticeable steepening. Ascend a L branch, really an independent scree ramp at nearly 40°, and after 100m. trend R over snow and rocks at an easier angle to the broad gully above the steep section. Follow the bed, steepening again, and exit R, away from Tadat above, to reach scree slopes which are crossed returning L (S) to the N foot of the tower, $2-2\frac{1}{2}$ h. from hut. Equally possible to exit by old zigzags up L side of gully hollow, steeper. Probably better mid season or later.

The easiest route starts on the shorter S side; the tower has been climbed by at least a dozen ways and variations, up to grade VI.

At the L side of the S face scramble broken ground to blocks, then climb a short chimney on L side of a large arrowhead; now go L up a cracked and slightly recessed narrow slabby ramp, finishing near the top of this by a short wall on R to reach a small shoulder on E side. Move L and finish up an easier chimney line to another small shoulder about 3m. under the summit. 20m., III-. J. de Lépiney, A. Stofer, 14 September, 1927. The big chimney on the longer N side is IV, strenuous.

TADAT COL c. 3740m.

In climbers' jargon, the saddle from which the Tadat tower rises. This has considerable value in providing a short if very rough passage between the Neltner and Lépiney huts. Neltner side, as above, $2\frac{1}{2}$ h. On the W side make a horizontal traverse SW just below the level of Tadat to reach rocks at base of N facet of Biguinoussene. By a little gully reach a screeband rising slightly and running R all the way to a small shoulder/col at the top of the sheer part of the latter's NW ridge. Descend the other side in a steep rock and scree couloir (snow) for 200m. into the hollow called Arzhane, being the highest cwm of the Azzaden valley immediately below the Tizi Melloul. Descend through the narrows below keeping to rocks on R side of bed, and at the bottom cross L before a stream gorge develops. By keeping to L side the Lépiney hut is soon reached, $2\frac{1}{4}$ h. from Tadat col, $3\frac{1}{4}$ h. in ascent. Grade I+.

AGUELZIM 3547m.

The gable N end of the Ouanoukrim chain. A few unsatisfactory rock climbs have been made on its flanks. Easy scrambling along the broad main ridge N from the Tadat col. It is possible to continue by the ridge to the Tizi n'Tizikert (2930m.) and over Adrar Adj (3129m.) to Imlil beyond; or descend steep slopes E to the Mizane valley and Sidi Chamharouch.

OUANOUKRIM CHAIN TRAVERSE

A long, entertaining and moderate rock scramble, the best of its kind in the region. By avoiding the central prongs of the Clochetons and taking a devious way round the Akioud towers it can be done at grade II-. Rather pointless because the few short pitches on or near the crest line are only grade II, or II+ for a few moves. Normally started or finished at the Tadat col. The N end of the chain to include Aguelzim involves for returning to the Neltner hut a reascent of the Mizane valley. From the route finding aspect easier in the direction S-N, from Neltner hut and back, coming down from the Tadat col, 11-14 h. without halts. Log book records traverses done in 8-9 h.

absence from hut. Sections not described under individual mountains above, in the S-N direction, are as follows:

<u>Akioud summits by SSE ridge from Tizi n'Bou Imrhaz.</u> From col descend on W side to make a slightly descending traverse on rubble under a prominent ridge thumb then the first ridge peaklet (this is IV, direct) to an inlet and gully mounting to the next ridge gap. To R of gully base climb a chimney (II) to a narrow ledge which can be walked L with some exposure to the gully bed above its initial pitch. Continue up bed to gap. Trend a little R of crest above and make a short traverse R into a gully on E side. Climb this to exit up a steep chimney (II+) followed by easy rocks to top of Akioud S. Now descend easily on R side of crest to gap in front of Akioud Central. From gap ascend steep firm rocks on R side of crest to top of Akioud Central. The wall below to next gap is IV+, or abseil. Avoid it by returning to previous gap, then make a descending traverse on W side below the rocks of Akioud Central, into a big scree gully which is ascended to the gap before Akioud N.

From the access col all this section can be avoided by a scree trundle below base of wall forming E side of ridge, going down then up, to cross steep scree extending to the gap of the Amguird n'Bou Imrhaz between Tadaft (q. v. above) and Akioud Central. From this col go up R into a loose gully with large boulders to attain gap between Akioud Central and North, I+.

Go up a fine wall on good holds trending L to a nice crack; take this to slabs leading pleasantly to top of Akioud N, II+. From col, by either route, $1\frac{1}{2}$ h.

<u>Afella N summit to the Clochetons and Biguinoussene.</u> From Afella N follow the easy crest with several little gaps to a shoulder above a short ridge step. Descend this direct (II-), or more easily by a circuit on E side. Continue along sharp crest with numerous little towers and gaps all straightforward to a tower overlooking a little saddle in front of the Clochetons.

Straight down the crest from here, moves of II+, avoidable on E side by going a short way down a gully and crossing a rib above it to reascend another gully emerging at the little saddle. This is normal exit from ravine below for parties coming up from Neltner hut. For the Clochetons, traverse or turn the first (S) prong easily on its E side and take the airy crest to below the twin central prongs. Climb a chimney (II+) to a narrow slot between the prongs. Bridge up the opening and at the top pull easily on to E and slightly lower top (II). A long stride across the void and a pull up lands you on the W prong. Descend the same way; either climb down W side of ridge before S prong to a ledge line (probably III), or return the same way to saddle before S prong; from there broken rock and scree on W side leads into a narrow horizontal terrace running across the rockface supporting the Clochetons, so that a prominent ridge gap further N can be entered easily. To attain the N prong, from slot between the central prongs, go along exposed ridge to its top, II-. Return same way. Note: from the S saddle and S prong a natural ledge line with chimney/gully interruptions can be followed across the E wall of all the prongs to gap at N end, II.

From the N end gap climb scree terraces on L (W) side to a steeper serrated crest which gives airy scrambling to a small rockhead before a gap and prominent square topped tower. Descend on L side to gap, or keep below it. (The tower ahead can be climbed by a chimney and traverse on its E side, III). Below the gap scree slopes are mounted directly to rock terraces and a steep ridge above the tower. Go up this in a fine position (II-) to the short summit crest and roof of Biguinoussene. All this section from Afella N, $3\frac{1}{2}$-4 h.

TIZI MELLOUL 3860m.

See under Afella and its W flank normal route, above, for approach from Neltner hut. The prominent saddle below the E edge of the Tazaghârt plateau and the depression between it and the W flank of the Ouanoukrim chain at the point where Afella is located. Topographically an important pass between the Azzaden and Agoundis valleys; chiefly used as an access point to its flanking summits.

From the Lépiney hut a small track mounts the R side of the valley and trends R under a buttress to below the Tazaghârt cliffs. Bear L above the head of a gorge and cross the stream to its L side, where another track, normally snow covered to mid June, works up boulder slopes in the gutter to finish steeply at the lower rim of the Arhzane cwm. Work up the bed of the hollow over bad ground and ascend very stony slopes at the back directly to the col, 3-3½ h.

TAZAGHÂRT   3974m.

Huge plateau summit, a characteristic geological sight in the High Atlas (e.g. Angour, Yagour, etc.), roughly rectangular and measuring over 2 x 1½ km. A barren, stone covered and windswept wilderness, the NE edge overlooking the Lépiney hut is supported by the most extensive and highest continuous cliffs (650m.) in the Toubkal region. The S side cliffs are less steep, more broken and remotely situated a long way above the Agoundis valley. At the E edge, the culminating point, the plateau flows into a steep ridge that drops to the Tizi Melloul. The W side fans out to broad slopes facing the Nfis valley. The normal route attains the Melloul pass and takes the ridge.

From Tizi Melloul. A rough scramble on loose rock, otherwise easy.

From the col (above), go up a broad staircase ridge, mostly scree, turning little steps on L side, sticking to the crest line as far as possible. Signal cairn at top, 30 min., 3½-4 h. from Lépiney hut. Coming from the Neltner hut by the Afella W flank route (q.v.), from where the col is reached in 15 min., much the same time.

Tazaghârt North-East Face

The main L (E) portion of this wall above the Lépiney hut is cut by a number of gullies divided by pronounced buttresses.

Its R flank is outlined by the Tsoukin (Tiskin, etc.) ridge. At the base of this stands the rockhead called Tsoukin (3325m., but probably 3290m.). On the other (W) side of the Tsoukin ridge lies the upper ravine called Amguerd nel Bordj, itself flanked on the W side by a big ridge spur coming off the Tazaghârt plateau and levelling out at the promontory of Aourir n'Irg (3171m.). The narrow section of cliff above the Bordj ravine has rarely repeated routes of 300m.

On the main cliff the principal features from L to R are: North-East Buttress 3938 (3900), Couloir de Neige, Tower Ridge 3874 (3830), Central Buttress, Diagonal Couloir, Arête Mediane, Descent Couloir, Tsoukin Ridge (3750). The figures are former traditional heights along the plateau rim (in parenthesis the more likely heights).

The classic route of the area is Couloir de Neige. It suffers from stonefall in early spring (is best done in winter). In spring and summer snow turned to black ice enhances difficulty. When comparatively bare and snowfree in late summer, rock pitches of IV can be quite unpleasant; grade IV in any season. The Diagonal Couloir is an excellent grade II in good snow conditions; nasty in mid season. All the buttresses have several routes from III to V, rock generally unsound. The ridges are better. Arête Mediane, which borders Diagonal Couloir, ranks high in interest and quality; IV with a key section in two pitches of V, variable. The Tsoukin ridge, III deviously, IV direct, has quite recent routes of V on its flanks. The Tsoukin rockhead offers numerous short technical climbs developed like a nursery hear the hut.

The Descent Couloir is the steep looking gully under the L (E) side of the Tsoukin ridge. The top can be difficult to locate from the plateau. In snow conditions climbing parties can come down it (I+) to the Lépiney hut in $1\frac{1}{2}$ h. Much the quickest way down to the hut. In summer and when snowfree it can be descended by walking parties with prudence and caution - very loose but not dangerous if taken steadily.

Tazaghârt outliers

The plateau zone eventually sinks and tapers into a broad ridge running SW to enclose the Agoundis valley down to Ijoukak. This ridge is easily reached by two high cols with mule paths for those starting from the latter valley. Coming from the Lépiney hut side the only practical course is to cross Tazaghârt and follow the ridge up and down over Ad. Iwzag-ner (Fouzar-har) (3490m.) and Makouz (3076m.). After descending to the Agoundis it would be possible to return over the Tizi Melloul by sleeping at the highest convenient huts or bivouacking. Alternatively over the Tizi n'Ouagane to the Neltner hut.

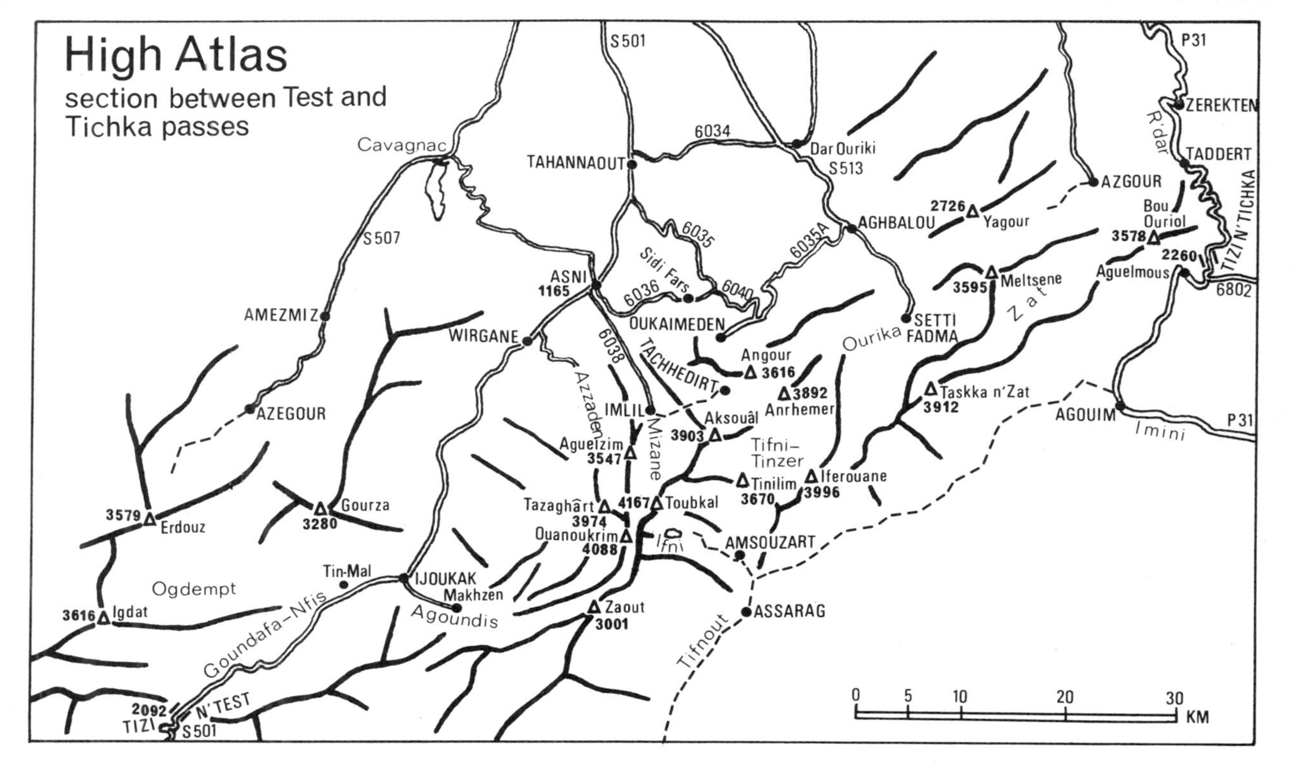

High Atlas
section between Test and Tichka passes
S 501
P31
ZEREKTEN
R'dar
TADDERT
Cavagnac
6034
Dar Ouriki
S 513
TAHANNAOUT
AZGOUR
TIZI N'TICHKA
2726
Yagour
Bou Ouriol
AGHBALOU
3578
S 507
6035
6035A
2260
Sidi Fars
6040
Meltsene
Aguelmous
ASNI
1165
6036
3595
6802
AMEZMIZ
OUKAIMEDEN
Ourika
SETTI FADMA
Zat
WIRGANE
6038
TACHHEDIRT
Angour
3616
Imini
AZEGOUR
Azzaden
IMLIL
Mizane
Aksouâl
3903
3892
Anrhemer
Taskka n'Zat
3912
AGOUIM
P31
Aguelzim
3547
Tifni–Tinzer
3579
Erdouz
Gourza
3280
Tazaghârt
4167
3974
Toubkal
Tinilim
3670
Iferouane
3996
Ouanoukrim
4088
Ifni
AMSOUZART
Tin-Mal
IJOUKAK
Ogdempt
Makhzen
3616
Igdat
Goundafa–Nfis
Agoundis
Zaout
3001
Tifnout
ASSARAG
2092
TIZI N'TEST
S 501
0 5 10 20 30 KM

AZROU N'TAMADÔT   3842m.

AKSOUÂL   3903m.

Companion summits of little topographical importance yet rank-
ing among the most sought after expeditions in the High Atlas.
The main ridge traverse between the two is one of the best
scrambles of its kind in the region. Tamadôt marks the junction
of the Aksouâl chain NNW ridge and the main Aksouâl-Iguen-
ouane ridge. This NNW ridge descends with complications to
the Tamatert col (2279m.) on the road between Imlil and Tacheddirt and has two important access cols in its meandering
length. All routes on these peaks tend to be long or steep or
both with screes worse than Toubkal. The laborious approach
slopes, especially on the N flank, may be climbed comfortably
with good snow cover; in these conditions crampons and mountaineering experience come into their own. All routes involve
a big vertical interval; underestimating height and distance to
be climbed, and the nature of the ground, has compelled many
unintentional bivouacs. First European ascent of Aksouâl: H.
Dolbeau, Marquis de Segonzac, 1922.

<u>South-West Ridge to Tamadôt (from Tizi n'Tagharât)</u>. The
recommended route for walkers; reaching the col is steeper
than anything encountered on the ridge. An axe should be carried if there is snow on the ridge (before mid May).

Imlil to Sidi Chamharouch, $2\frac{1}{4}$ h. (Neltner hut trail). Sidi
to the Tagharat col (q.v.), 4 h. Possible to sleep in Berber
house at Sidi, or camping on a large platform above Mizane
river 50m. beyond hamlet. A camp or bivouac on the broad
col, no water, might be uncomfortable due to prevailing strong
wind. Porter or mule hire convenient to this point.

From the Tizi n'Tagharât (3442m.) ascend easy stone slopes
N on R side of crest line to a shoulder (3664m., somewhat
above the summit proper of Ad. Agouti), and continue along
broad ridge to mount a little step then a rocky peaklet, Db.
Tagharât, beyond which the undulating crest attains a rocky
shoulder, called Epaule (3770m.) by the French. From this
point the ridge gathers into a series of fine towers which can
be climbed or partly turned by numerous pitches of II and III.
The walking route descends steep rubble for 80m. on the R (S)

side of the ridge, then works R below a rockband to gain a little shoulder.   Above this ascend a scree slope half L to another, broad shoulder.   Continue the same line in a rising traverse over scree and blocks to an obvious ridge saddle just above the last towers, then follow the easy crest to a forepeak. Reach the main summit of Tamadôt in a few min., $1\frac{1}{2}$ h. from col. Climbing parties should add 2 h. for going over the ridge towers.

<u>From Aroumd</u>. Above the village an obvious side valley rises E with progressive steepness and divides at 2500m. The L brance leads to the Arhzane col (see below) then the summit. Very tedious terrain, continuously steep above 3000m., small track, not easy to find, below this level. Shepherd's hut at 2600m. 6 h.

<u>North Side Route to Tamadôt by the Irhzer n'Temda</u>.   The easiest and most direct way from Tacheddirt hut. Steep scree slopes and broken rock, technically easy. For experienced walkers, June onwards. Interesting and straightforward with frozen snow, in crampons. Average angle above the central hollow is 36°, reaching 40° at top of gully.

From Tacheddirt hut take the main trail through village; halfway along, between two houses on R, a track forks R to descend and cross the river. Follow this trail back R above river between damp fields directly below the valley running up to the Likemt col. Having crossed its outflow leave the track and make an ascending traverse round grassy slopes into the next side valley and go up its bed by a track on L side to where it divides (pt. 2400m.). The gully/ravine to R leads straight up to the Arhzane col (3614m.), a gap nearly at the top of the NNW ridge.   Follow the stony bed to narrows twisting R and scramble rocks to the lower end of a hollow still lying at a good angle.   A narrow ravine forks L. Continue straightahead to

steep broken rocks closing upper end of hollow. Turn these
rocks L then R to rejoin the bed. Now follow the consistently
steep and quite narrow gully, hemmed in by impressive rock
scenery, to emerge at the Arhzane gap, $4\frac{1}{4}$ h. From here
ascend rubble/snow under some ridge towers then trend R over
blocks to reach the SW forepeak of the mountain. Follow main
ridge L to top, 45 min. , 5 h. from hut.

<u>East-North-East Ridge to Aksouâl (from Tizi n'Likemt)</u>. The
normal route, fairly long and monotonous but perfectly easy.
A bivouac on the col might be desirable (porter and mule hire
at Tacheddirt) though it is a bleak and waterless place in summer.

From Tacheddirt to col as described in the Mountain Huts
section, $3\frac{1}{2}$-4 h. From the Tizi n'Likemt (3540m.) follow the
crest over three small summits to a more rocky and narrow
section where little gaps are easily turned L. Higher up two
or three small teeth can be climbed or turned L or R to reach
a large rockhead (3776m.). Descend keeping slightly L to a
ridge saddle, Col de l'Azib (3710m.), where the direct route
from Tacheddirt exits. A typical broken narrow crest beyond
is scrambled to another, larger rockhead, becoming broad and
horizontal, where snow may lie to mid season. Finally a short
step taken by a rough slope on the L to a forepeak, to return R
by a simple ridge to the summit, $3\frac{1}{4}$ h. from col, about $7\frac{1}{4}$ h.
from Tacheddirt.

<u>North Side Direct Route.</u> A technically easy (I+) but compli-
cated ascent of the ravine called Irhzer n'Ouksoual, rising to
the Col de l'Azib in the ENE ridge. At the fork 2400m. described in previous route but one, the ravine is the main L
branch. After an entry section its lower gorge is avoided by a
parallel incision R. In the multiple gully system halfway up
you keep L under rock walls, to finish trending R with an

unsuspected exit L. Quite difficult route finding. Tacheddirt
to Col de l'Azib, about 5 h., total time to summit, $5\frac{3}{4}$ h.

Tamadôt-Aksouâl Main Ridge. The two summits are separated
by the col of the Amguerd n'Ouksoual (3740m.). From here
the ridge to Aksouâl is fairly short and broken, keeping R (S)
in ascent, 45 min. To Tamadôt it is serrated and marked by
the several picturesque Aksouâl towers. The direct traverse
of these gives an exposed and satisfying rock climb of grade
III-; the highest tower has sustained difficulties at this level.
$1\frac{1}{2}$ h. J. de Lépiney, A. Stofer, 22 June, 1928. Ridge traversers can conveniently avoid the towers in two ways. From
the saddle between the two tops of Tamadôt descend steep scree
or snow below the S side of the towers and traverse horizontally, crossing two narrow gullies, to rise slightly and rejoin
the ridge about 200m. distance from the Ouksoual col. Do not
try to traverse directly to the col - very loose and steep, 30-
45 min. Or, from the saddle between the two tops make a
descending traverse under the N side cliff of the main summit
to follow a broad ledge, descending slightly then running horizontally below the towers to join the ridge at the same place
as the S side variation. Exposed, a few narrow points, easy
but not advisable when snow covered, 30 min.

North Side Climbing Routes. The discontinuous buttresses
and spurs divided by a system of complex ravines and gullies
have all been climbed by routes rarely exceeding grade IV.
Some of the rock is good for long stretches while a lot is poor.
The terminal escarpment wall of Aksouâl is IV, direct. That
of Tamadôt, above the ledgeband, III+. Both are 100m. The
longest general mountaineering route on this side is the NNE
ridge, in line with the Ouksoual col, 1200m., mostly I+ with a
few pitches of II/II+.

BOU IGUENOUANE   3882m.

A mountain that vies with Toubkal for displaying the worst
screes in the world. A walker's slag heap par excellence, always better with snow cover above 3000m. to obliterate the
curses of loose stony ground. Normally snow disappears rapidly after end May.

<u>North Side Normal Route (Amazzer Meqqoren)</u>.   Perfectly
visible from the Tacheddirt hut all the way up to a large saddle
L (E) of the summit area. This Amazzer is the valley with a
stream flowing in several pretty cascades. Its upper trackless
slopes are bad scree with no obstacles whatever.

From Tacheddirt start as for the Tizi Likemt (q. v.) and go
into the side valley a few min. after crossing the river. A
track keeps L over rough grass slopes to reach the bed above
the first cascade. Now cross to R side and follow up the bed,
small track, to scree slopes. Mount these somewhat R, away
from the bed, to enter a huge hollow with old moraines curving
down it.   Follow the main L hand moraine at an easy angle,
gradually bending L into plain scree and boulder slopes, snow
covered to mid May. Ascend these long slopes directly to the
skyline saddle at the top, the best walking line always trending
slightly L (3730m.), $4\frac{1}{2}$ h.   Bear R (SW) and ascend similar
slope away from the crest line to reach by moving L then R a
preliminary dome; finally by the main ridge to summit at the
far end, 30 min., 5 h. from Tacheddirt.

<u>West-South-West Ridge (from Tizi n'Likemt)</u>. Normally taken
in descent. Even more tedious though shorter than its counter-
part to Aksouâl.

From the Tizi n'Likemt (q. v.) above Tacheddirt ascend to
a large scree knoll (3615m.) then descend over a broad saddle
and follow the continuation ridge with a few teeth turned R to
reach a narrow crest at a little ridge summit. The next section
developes as a series of towers which can be traversed at grade
III to a gap before the final ridge; not particularly interesting.

102

Avoid this section by descending on the S side and contouring below the towers over steep debris slopes cut by several gullies to rejoin the ridge by a gully going up to the pinnacled last gap. Keeping R, ascend the moderately steep rock ridge to top, $2\frac{1}{2}$ h. from col, $6\frac{1}{2}$ h. from Tacheddirt, 4 h. in descent.

<u>North Ridge</u>. As easy as any route, but longer than most. The approach co-incides with Anrhemer normal route. See comments about the Tacheddirt col in Mountain Huts section.

From the Tizi n'Tacheddirt (3172m.) ascend a stony grass slope due S to a rockband. Turn this L up a vague ramp and return R towards crest of broad spur. Cross a low rockband to reach a larger one which is also turned on L side to rejoin the ridge line. Now follow up just L of crest, vague track in places, getting more rocky, to where the angle eases off and the spur ahead merges into broken rocks. Traverse L to a vague parallel rib and go up this in the same line to steep blocks with good ledges. Turn a finger rock on the R and ascend trending R to debris leading out to an obvious saddle in the main ridge at the foot of Anrhemer. <u>Tizi n'Tigourzatine</u> (3680m.), $1\frac{3}{4}$ h.

Turn R over rubble and climb a short gully to a rockhead. Descend from this on broken rock keeping L (E) under a gap and pyramid then traverse to a huge screefield in a saddle. Continue up broad ridge on scree/snow to the secondary summit of <u>Ad. nou Ahior</u> (3790m.). Descend similar slopes to the saddle reached by the North Side route, and continue thus to top, $2\frac{3}{4}$ h., $4\frac{1}{2}$ h. from Tacheddirt col, 7 h. from Tacheddirt hut.

ANRHEMER   3892m.

Ad. n'Ineghmar. A rock peak on all sides. Just about the only major summit in the Toubkal region that might be considered too adventurous for walkers. Less effort and better walking ground than Aksouâl and Iguenouane. The N face, while

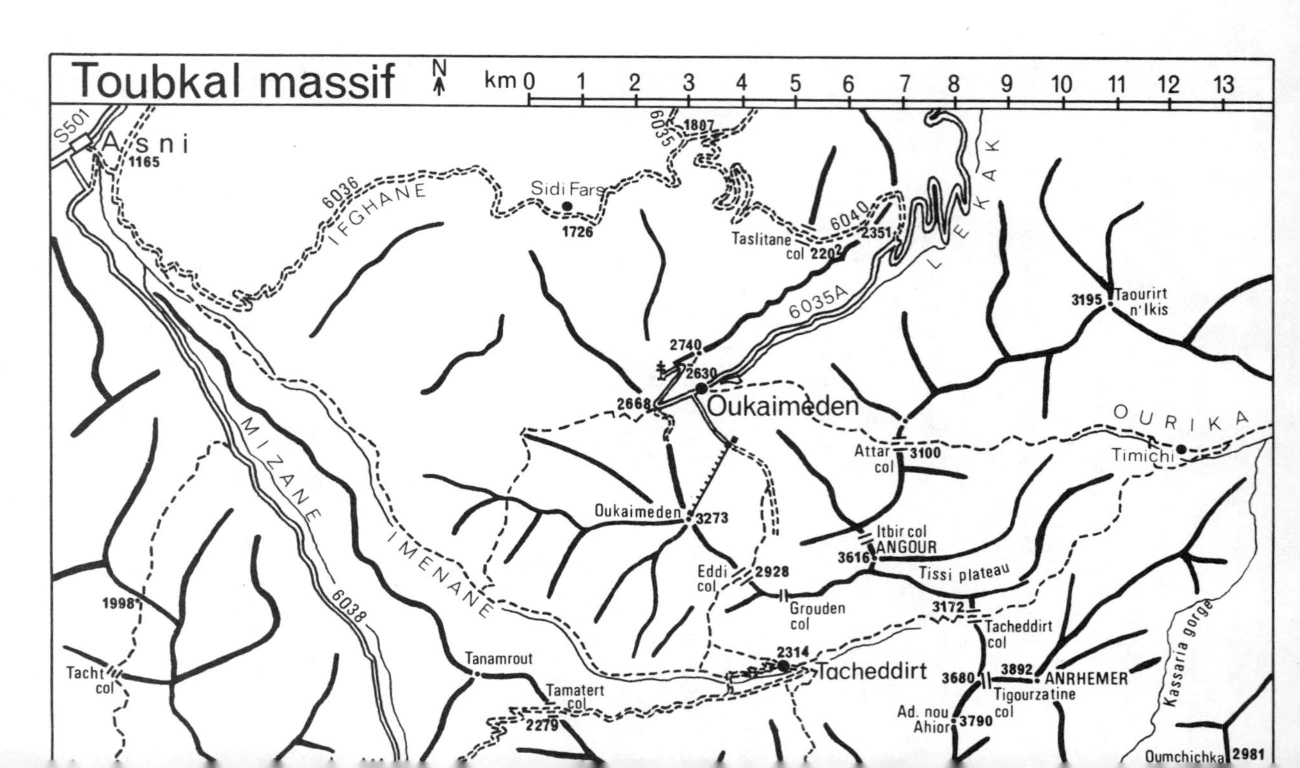

Toubkal massif
N
km 0 1 2 3 4 5 6 7 8 9 10 11 12 13
S501
Asni
1165
6036
IFGHANE
6035
1807
Sidi Fars
1726
Taslitane col 2202
6040
2351
LEKAK
3195 Taourirt n'Ikis
6035A
2740
2630
2668
Oukaimeden
OURIKA
Attar col 3100
Timichi
MIZANE
IMENANE
6038
Oukaimeden 3273
Itbir col
ANGOUR
3616
Tissi plateau
Eddi col 2928
Grouden col
3172
Tacheddirt col
1998
Tanamrout
Tamatert col
2279
Tacht col
2314
Tacheddirt
3680
3892 ANRHEMER
Tigourzatine col
Ad. nou Ahior 3790
Kassaria gorge
Oumchichka 2981

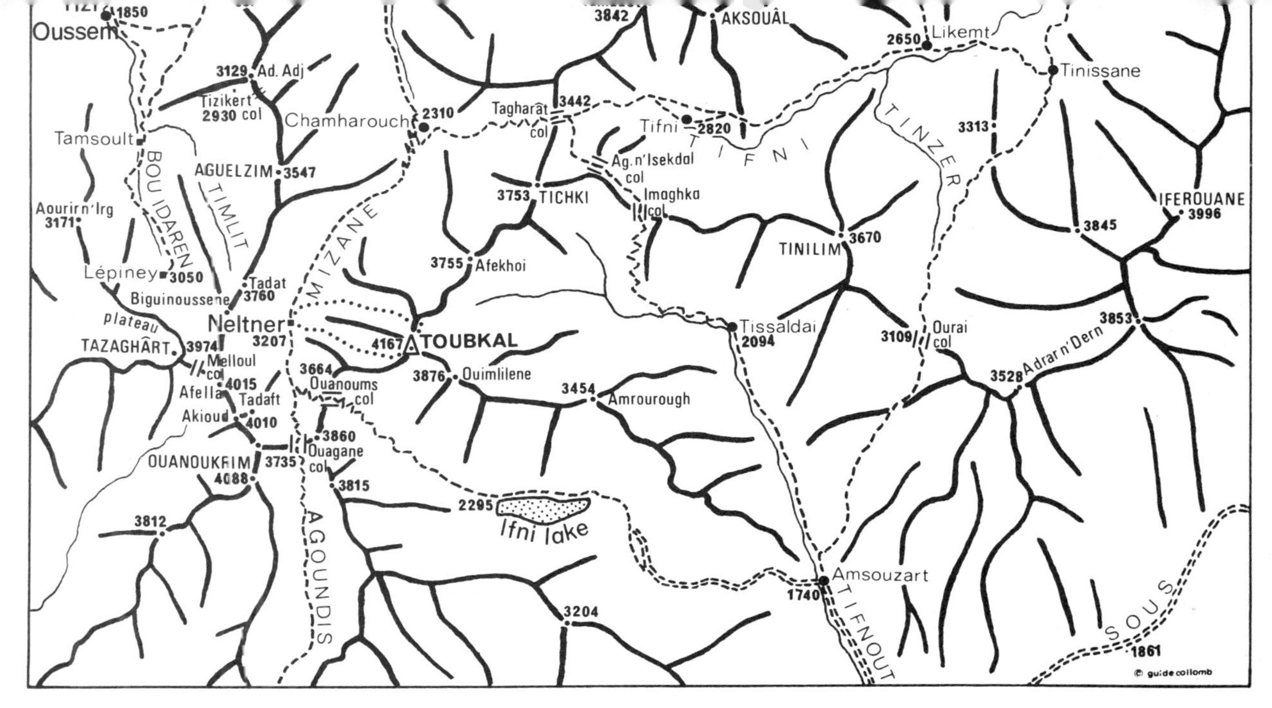

Oussem
TIZI-n 1850
Tamsoult
Aourir n'Irg 3171
3129 Ad. Adj
Tizikert 2930 col
BOU IDAREN
TIMLIT
AGUELZIM 3547
Lépiney 3050
Biguinoussene
plateau
Neltner 3207
TAZAGHÂRT 3974
Melloul col
Afella 4015
Tadat 3760
Tadaft
Akioud 4010
OUANOUKRIM 4088
3735
Ouagane col
3860
3815
3812
MIZANE
Chamharouch 2310
Tagharât col 3442
TICHKI 3753
Ag. n'Isekdal col
Imaghka col
Afekhoi 3755
TOUBKAL 4167
3664
Ouanoums col
Ouimlilene 3876
3454 Amrourough
AGOUNDIS
3204
2295
Ifni lake
3842
AKSOUÂL
Tifni 2820
TIFNI
TINILIM 3670
Tissaldai 2094
2650 Likemt
Tinissane
TINZER
3313
IFEROUANE 3996
3845
3109 Ourai col
3853
3528 Adrar n'Dern
Amsouzart 1740
TIFNOUT
SOUS
1861
© guide collomb

impressive, is too broken to offer satisfactory technical climbing. There are noted rockfaces on the E and S sides (900m., grade IV), above the Tifni (Kassaria) gorge, remotely situated and rarely climbed. The main ridge traverse integral involves an awkward reascent over the Tacheddirt col unless done in the reverse direction, from Setti Fadma. First European ascent: M. de Prandières, June, 1925.

<u>West Ridge.</u> The usual and shortest route from any starting point. Quite pleasant with nice situations reserved for the last 30 min. Several pitches of grade I.

From Tacheddirt to the Tizi n'Tacheddirt (q. v.), $2\frac{1}{2}$ h., then to the Tizi n'Tigourzatine (3680m.), as for the previous route, $1\frac{3}{4}$ h. From this col turn up the ridge keeping to a series of obvious outward sloping and large ramps rising parallel with the W ridge below its crest on R (S) side. These lead without incident, and normally snowfree after end April, to the W summit (3885m.). Now follow the level crest with two little rock steps to an intermediate summit overlooking a fairly deep gap. Descend on the crest over broken rock, turning short obstacles L, to the gap. This is double, with an interesting scramble over two knobs and a turning movement L round a gendarme into notch under the last steep ridge step. Go up this direct to a little shoulder then follow the ragged crest or keep slightly L to a tiny gap and the summit mound above, $1\frac{1}{2}$ h. from Tigourzatane col, $5\frac{3}{4}$ h. from Tacheddirt hut.

<u>North-East Ridge.</u> A fine mountaineering expedition, awkward of access and normally taken in descent. Some route finding ability needed on the upper part to avoid pitches of III. Shorter version, described below, grade II-.

In descent, from summit follow broad broken crest keeping L to slabs and a step. Follow crest down over three steep pitches to a wall above a gap. Take an exposed ramp on N side slanting into a steep loose gully, and by this return under wall below the gap. Cross gully below gap and climb the easy retaining wall to a prominent rockhead above gap. Descend

a rockband under N side of ridge to a small hollow and go down
this along a narrow rake, under the nose, to reascend and join
the crest again on a narrow ridge shoulder. Continue by the
fine crest to a step above a gap containing a small tooth. Follow
crest down keeping slightly L to gap. Quit the ridge at this
point (c. 3450m.) and go down a large scree rake on N side into
a big gully. Descend this on debris until it is possible to traverse L (W) under the N face of the mountain from where easy
ground is crossed to regain the Tacheddirt col, 2 h. All this
section from the ridge retains snow until mid season.

Parties continuing further down the ridge, to pt. 2886m.,
have very rough ground to descend and cross in order to rejoin
the Tacheddirt col path on the Ourika side.

ANGOUR   3616m.

One of the most popular peaks in the area. The ascent from
the Oukaimeden (N) side is for experienced walkers or rock
scramblers. The easiest route goes up in a long circuit from
Tacheddirt via the Tissi plateau. The latter is a huge sloping
plain of poor grass and stones, $2\frac{1}{2}$ x 1 km. in extent, forming
the E flank of the mountain. Berbers graze sheep and goats
there from early spring. The summit is double, a S top standing precisely at the head of the plateau and a N top, slightly
higher, isolated by a gap and sheer rock walls on the W and N
sides.

<u>North Side Ledge and Gully.</u>   The shortest and easiest way
from Oukaimeden.   Exposed by walking standards, steep
scrambling pitches. Grade I.

From Oukaimeden approach by road passing chairlift station
and follow the lorry road in valley bed to the spoil tips at end.
Same as for Tizi n'Ouadi, q. v., 45 min., possible for cars.
From here work L (E) and go up the valley rising below the
craggy NW face of Angour. A small track winds up the R side
then the L side of the bed, in the upper part in zigzags on steep
scree to reach the obvious saddle at top, <u>Tizi n'Itbir</u> (3295m.),
$1\frac{1}{2}$ h.   Above is the steep N buttress, good routes for nearly
250m. in grades III & IV.

From the col ascend scree to an open gully on R flank of buttress. Climb it slanting R into narrows, and avoid several slab pitches by moving R. Above, follow the bed and trending L, exit L at a gap in the N buttress nearly halfway up to summit. On the far side of the gap a ledge line goes off L across the N face between sheer rock walls and runs more or less horizontally to exit in the NE couloir which marks the L side of the buttress area. This couloir (which can also be climbed more tediously from the bottom) leads up easily over shelves of steep scree to the summit plateau. Pass below the rock mound of the summit and enter an obvious gap on its L (W) side. Cross gap, stepping L then R, and slant steeply R up a wall with good holds to top, 2 h., $4\frac{1}{4}$ h. from Oukaimeden ($3\frac{1}{2}$ h. for motorists).

West Ridge. The classic route, rarely climbed from the Tacheddirt side owing to exceedingly steep and tiresome approach slopes. This long ridge is joined at the Tizi n'Grouden (3090m.), a scree saddle directly above but invisible from Tacheddirt. It occurs about one km. after the Ouadi col, and is separated from the latter by a lower craggy extension of the W ridge. The approach from Oukaimeden is nearly as steep but shorter. The upper rocky stretches of ridge give several short sections of grade I, most of which can be avoided by good route finding.

From Oukaimeden as for the Tizi n'Ouadi (q.v.), or as the previous route, to lorry roadhead, 45 min. (carparking). Go into the main narrows ahead, on L side of stream, and once round the corner R (5 min.) a moraine like feature appears on L, just past the natural entrance to the cwm overhead and below the Grouden col. Ascend loose scree up this flank at the only point not closed by small cliffs. Continue, trackless, up R side of cwm, keeping R in a series of zigzags, crossing two or three scrub spurs; higher up, where the angle steepens, keep even further R to avoid rockbands, and finally resume a direct ascent with a small track in parts. Reach a spur which can be followed half R, then leave it for a rising traverse half L to reach the Grouden col, $1\frac{1}{4}$ h.

Go up broad ridge and ascend a broken facet direct, loose, to a rockhead; ruined track. Continue, keeping slightly L and pass below a little crag to join a rock slope where the ridge blends into the rough SW flank of the mountain. Directly above is the W ridge crest proper which falls down as a rock spur enclosing the L (E) side of the Grouden cwm just ascended. At top of rock slope grassy terraces lead upward and R to base of a prominent cliff and a horizontal ledge on R, cairn. Go round corner R and climb a shallow green caterpillar groove direct, bits of a track, alongside sub wall of cliff, 35° steep for 100m. to ridge at top, small grassy saddle platform, $1\frac{1}{4}$ h. Go along rocky ridge, on crest or L side to a broader section. Follow this avoiding two knolls on L to rejoin crest which is taken into a small rock gap. The chimney above is I+ direct. Climb it for 3m. then move L into an easy hidden groove, from which you exit L in another 5m. From rock strewn slope above take the next ridge step on R side, poor track; after this the entire ridge is followed by the crest or movements on L side. It narrows progressively and becomes rocky. Turn small steps as desired, often loose, up to a larger double step. The first is II- direct, recommended; or turn it in a fairly wide circular movement L, latterly up loose grassy rocks (I); the second should be followed on or near crest. A serrated edge now leads with interest to a rockhead from where a scratched rock groove (I), not avoidable, is descended just R (S) of crest for 20m. to a scree/snow saddle; end of ridge. Two knolls above mark edge of Tissi plateau. Make a rising traverse L to cross a slight shoulder on the L outline halfway up the L hand knoll. Continue traversing at a lower angle to the plateau rim ahead. This last section from scree saddle overlooks exit from the impressive NW gully which arrives at same place from depths below. Go up plateau to S summit at top. Follow broad ridge R then easy slabs into gap before the main N summit, and finish as for previous route, $1\frac{1}{4}$ h., $4\frac{1}{2}$ h. from Oukaimeden ($3\frac{3}{4}$ h. for motorists).

Parties can descend from the Grouden col to Tacheddirt by scree and broken rock, and a ravine, all at an average angle of 35° and very unpleasant, 1 h.

East Flank (Tissi Plateau). A roundabout route, the normal one from Tacheddirt, easy.

From the Tizi n'Tacheddirt (q. v.) ascend rough grass slope due N of col to its highest point against rocks. Move R for 50m. to a ramp line slanting back L. Follow this to a low rockband under plateau and go up it at one of several easy points, 45 min. Now work along broad ridge forming top of the S face cliffs; a ridge is formed here because the plateau is cut longitudinally by a deep ravine on this S side which peters out eventually some distance from the top. The ridge is a walk with a few gaps of no consequence; the last and deepest marks the exit of East Gully in the S face. Above this take a steep rock strewn slope slightly R to join the plateau above its ravine. Continue up the plateau, keeping some 100m. distance from the rim of the S face and go directly into gap between the twin summits to finish as for the previous routes, 2 h., $4\frac{1}{2}$ h. from Tacheddirt.

South Face   This very extensive cliff, about 2 km. wide, rises imposingly above the Tacheddirt col mule trail and reaches in places a height of 400m. (see illus.). More than a dozen climbs have been made, some of which still await second ascents. In fact rarely visited by rock climbers. While none of the features comprising this face are particularly pronounced - due to broken and discontinuous areas of rock - the following detail enables it to be examined in broad parts. A fairly central gully depression divides it equally; this gully has two branches in the upper half. Further R an East Gully divides the cliff again. This gully is obvious from the top (see previous route) but is hard to identify from below. To L of Central Gully a Western Groove runs the full height of the face. The extreme L side of the face is marked by a relatively short gully. The extreme R peters out in short rockbands and terraces above the Tacheddirt col. L of Western Groove the cliff is marked along the top by the W ridge; to the R of that by the Tissi plateau which lower down gives way to the ridge described in previous route. The rock is often poor but improves with steepness.

Bentley Beetham climbed the face by the Central Gully in 1927. He also went up the cliff in the neighbourhood of Western Groove. Face routes were climbed by the French in the 1930s. From L to R, Gendarme Ridge, bordering L side of far L gully (III). The buttress on R side of this gully has the original 150m. chimney route (IV) and two modern routes of V. From here all the area up to Western Groove is very broken. Between the latter and Central Gully climbs of 400m. in grades IV/V+ have been made. A long mountaineering route can be followed up the varied buttress on immediate R of Central Gully; 400m., III. Halfway up, parallel triple buttresses make it infinitely variable, with at least one good line of V+. The wall between these buttresses and East Gully has been climbed. The buttress bounding R side of latter gully has a challenging central mass of rock with a conspicuous White Ridge section towards the top (IV). Several climbs of a higher standard hereabouts.

OUKAIMEDEN   3273m.

An excellent viewpoint, well worth walking up despite the chair-lift option. The most direct way follows the grassy N ridge from the Tizrag col at SW end of the resort. Jeep road partway up this ridge, 2 h. Alternatively, and recommended for descent, a good track starts from near the point where the Ouadi col trail branches from the lorry road; this track works up a grassy valley in E side of the mountain to reach summit at top, $2\frac{3}{4}$ h. in ascent.

IFEROUANE   3996m.

Not named on 100m. map. An enormous hulk ascended by de Segonzac in 1922 in error for the highest point in the Toubkal massif, and a red-herring exercise ever since for many determined 4000m. peak baggers who also made the effort only to see the summit revised downwards in 1964 from former measurements of 4003 and 4001m. to a level below the magic mark.

A fairly distinct subsidiary dome (3930m.) for this whaleback ridge is formed one km. SW of the long summit elevation, from which broad multiple spurs descend from or near pt. 3845m. into the Tifni-Tinzer basin. Spurs like arms converge in the lower part of a tributary valley system immediately above the Tinissane huts (2720m.), see Tifni-Tinzer basin in Mountain Huts section. All three spurs give walking routes of 4 to 6 km. The central one is most direct, but steep and loose at the top. On average, 6 h. to summit from Tinissane huts. See photo diagram.

ADRAR N'DERN   3853m.

Huge rounded summit about 3 km. S of Iferouane, its name synonymous with the Berber name for the Toubkal region. No interest.

ADRAR TINILIM   3670m.

Given undue prominence on all maps, easily climbed by its long N ridge from the Likemt huts (Tifni-Tinzer basin, in Mountain Huts section) in $4\frac{1}{2}$ h., or from the trail over the Tizi n'Ourai (3109m.), by S ridge in 2 h., or $4\frac{1}{2}$ h. from Tinissane huts.

Outlying Summits

<u>Siroua</u>   3305m.

Sirwa on latest maps. Remotely situated, this extinct volcano constitutes a minor expedition in itself. The best approach is by a jeep road going NE from Taliwine on the P.32. This road is strictly for jeep type vehicles, bad surface, narrow and potholded. Possible to hire a vehicle and driver at Taliwine. The road joins another similar "piste track" at Askaoun (35 km.), running W-E from Aoulouz to Anezal across the high plateau country forming the great arid depression between Siroua and the Toubkal massif outliers. This transversal road is followed for 11 km. to a sharp bend at the Magous valley gorge. Vehicle parked here at 2450m. All provisions should be carried in, and after April, water.

A track at a higher level penetrates S above the gorge and is followed to a saddle at the top; then a descent of 200m. to the head of another valley under NW side of mountain. From here the summit can be reached directly up the NW spur over pt. 2886m. but the upper part is very loose. Alternatively, cross the N base of the mountain by a track leading on to a saddle between Siroua and Tikniwine (2952m.). From here take the NE spur at an easy angle to top. The last 50m. from any direction is a cone of very rotten rock at N end of summit ridge. 7 km., $5\frac{1}{2}$-$6\frac{1}{2}$ h. from jeep road.

Gourza   3280m.

Large scrub covered mountain above the Test pass road near Ijoukak.   A deep S cwm is followed by a mule trail to the Tizi n'Imiri (2855m.), then the rounded WSW ridge, about $5\frac{1}{2}$ h. from road at Mzouzit.   Or from the nearby Tin-Mal mosque a trail mounts the S spur of pt. 2913m. to join the E ridge which is followed to top, $4\frac{1}{2}$ h.

Erdouz   3579m.

Frequented by walkers for half a century; possible from Marrakech in a day with a very early start; much more relaxed with an overnight halt.

North side normal route.   Marrakech-Amezmiz, frequent bus service along S. 507, 54 km. Amezmiz, all main services; from here by twisty metalled road to Azegour, then rather rough but easy road to its head at the Erdouz lead mines (2150m.).   Berber inn, some provisioning, camping possible, 28 km. from Amezmiz.   This site is dominated by the N flank of the mountain.

Follow mule trail alongside stream in valley to mine workings with service cableway (2600m.).   The trail returns above E side of valley then moves back to ascend in many zigzags beside a secondary stream which is quitted for open slopes heading due S to the main ridge which is reached at the Tizi n'Louez (3280m.).   Follow broad ridge over a subsidiary summit to main one, 6 h.

A more direct alternative, somewhat steeper, is to leave mule trail before the upper mine workings and continue in main valley bed on L side.   Cross to R side after 300m. and move R on to broad spur.   Follow this to top then go along a saddle and up the steep N ridge, 5-$5\frac{1}{2}$ h.   The stream bed could be followed all the way into an upper couloir exiting on N ridge to save 30 min.

From the Test pass road a fairly long two-day expedition. Mule hire, inquire at Ijoukak. Dh. 30.00 per day in 1979. On main road below Mzouzit a mule trail goes W up the winding and endless Ogdempt valley, through successive walnut groves and hamlets to Areg (Arg) at the top, 2150m., $6\frac{1}{2}$-7 h. Sleeping in Berber huts or camping.   From Areg a mule trail N crosses two intervening ridges to reach the Tizi n'Tighfist (2895m.).   Above this col steep slopes lead up a depression to pt. 3367m. marking the end of Erdouz SW ridge.   Follow this broad easy ridge at a moderate angle for 2 km. to top, $5\frac{1}{2}$ h. from Areg.

<u>Igdat</u>   3616m.

Massive elevation with ravine eroded slopes on all flanks. Superb panorama, much frequented by natives but still rarely by
visitors.   From the Test pass road, as for Erdouz above, to
Areg, overnight halt.   From this hamlet an excellent mule
trail mounts to the Tizi n'Oumslma (3045m.) where the broad
and grassy then rocky N ridge is taken with a small track to a
broad shoulder followed by the summit, 5 h. from Areg.

OURIKA AREA

<u>Taskka n'Zat</u>   3912m.

This great summit lies at the head of the long Zat valley by
which it can be approached in two days on foot. Mules can
only go to 2000m. , and more convenient tactics are as follows.
   From a base at Setti Fadma, q.v. , inns, etc. , take porters
with local knowledge to carry up the Louah valley E and follow
the small rough track over the ridge at the Tizi n'Tilst
(c. 2800m.) to drop down into the upper Zat. Good site beside
the stream higher up at pt. 2467m. for camping or bivouac,
about 6 h. from Setti Fadma.
   From this point go further up valley to foot of N ridge of
mountain. Ascend this with steep rock scrambling to top,
5-6 h. Associated summits of just under 3900m. rise on the
main ridge running W from the main E top, the descent from
which is grade I to gap before the second; a round could be
made over these to descend from the top of the valley where
the exit slopes are moderate and hold snow until midsummer.
Similarly this round could be prolonged on the N side to Arjoût
(3741m.).

<u>Arjoût</u>   3741m.

A way up the very steep forest directly above Setti Fadma can
doubtless be made to follow one or other of the two arms com-
posing the N spur of this mountain. No other information.

<u>Meltsenc</u>   3595m.

A renowned pyramid summit straddling the divide between the
Ourika and Zat valleys. The Zat (SE) slopes are uncomfortably
steep; the Berber pastoral highway across the Rhellis depression between Meltsene and the Yagour plateau is much the

best starting point for going up the relatively gentle NW slopes.
The SW ridge can be climbed directly from Setti Fadma with a
hard approach to its moderate middle crest and fine rocky
upper, in 7 h. from the highest huts.

From the road below Setti Fadma a rough stony mule trail
mounts above the E side of the Ourika from pt. 1249m. in a
gorge to the hill farming zone of Anammer, and continues to
the lower edge of the Yagour plateau. This trail leads to the
lower Iferd huts, then a track is taken S towards Meltsene for
2 km. to the upper huts (2400m.). Accommodation with ob-
liging Berbers, 11 km., $4\frac{1}{2}$ h. from road.

From here the route is simply up the stream bed with a
small track to a large stonefield sloping gradually to the summit head, $4\frac{1}{2}$-5 h. The NW ridge is more interesting and
steeper. From the upper Iferd huts ascend a broad spur SW
at an easy angle; it narrows to a rocky crest which is followed
to pt. 3107m. on the NW ridge. The crest leads with increasing
steepness to a prominent shoulder, then a saddle and a rocky
terminal ridge whose steps are easily turned L up to a promontory marking the buttress head where the NW and SW ridges
unite. A simple ridge remains to the top, $5\frac{1}{2}$ h.

Adrar Yagour   2726m.

Opposite and parallel with the Meltsene ridge, an immense
plateau zone, and largest and most characteristic of these curious landforms in the High Atlas, measuring overall 12 x 4 km.
A magnificent summer pasture for the Berber community. The
rock inscriptions referred to in the Valley Bases section of
the guide are found among the parallel rockbands NNE of the
Amddouz huts. The trail to Meltsene (above) passes 100m.
below them.

ZAT - TICHKA AREA

The Zat valley, branching from the Marrakech-Tichka col road
near Taferiate, is motorable to Azgour hamlet (1350m.).
Sleeping in Berber houses, or camping, no bus service, taxi
possible, limited provisioning at Arba Tighedouine (given other
names) lower down. Parties relying on public transport are
recommended to use the frequent bus service along the main
P.31 road. Get off below Taddert at Tazlida (Ait Mançour);
small inn, café, Berber shops. From here a broad pathway
ascends terraced cultivations W over the Tizi n'Leilat (1761m.)
to descend by various hamlets into the Zat valley at Mriouat.
From here go up the main valley for $\frac{1}{2}$ km. to cross the Zat
river by a rickety bridge below Ait Slimane, where the rough

motor road is joined that leads to Azgour, about 4 h.

<u>Bou Ouriol</u>   3578m.

Adrar Tircht on latest 100m. map. Huge mountain dominating
head of the Zat valley intermediate bend, and commanding the
western heights above the Tichka pass road.   Its generally
broad ridges radiate like the spokes of a wheel. The E ridge,
with a prominent branch low down forking NE, and the main
NE ridge run down to the Tichka pass road. The SW ridge
runs off from a SE forepeak called Isk n'Yahia, and this ridge
drops to a broad saddle (3171m.) before rising again to the
Ad. Oulaounine (3421m.).   A N ridge twists down with rock
scarps on its E side to a valley depression marking all the N
base of the mountain; this depression carries a rough jeep
road and mule trail from the Tichka pass road at pt. 2076m.
('refuge'on map)to the Zat valley at Ait Slimane (by this route
to Azgour, about 5 h.).   The main W ridge falls gradually to
Tizert hamlet (1479m.) at the big bend in the Zat valley narrows
some distance above Azgour.
   Ascent routes from the Zat side are fairly long if tried without an intermediate bivouac, but easy. From Azgour approach
by a short day to Tidsi hamlet (1721m.) in the valley depression
midway between Ait Slimane and the Tichka road. From here
take the N ridge, quite rocky in the top part, to summit in
$6\frac{1}{2}$ h.
   Routes from the Tichka pass road are easy and can be started
from the building marked 'refuge' (2076m.) on map, good
campsite; from here work directly up the NE ridge to summit,
about $5\frac{1}{2}$-6 h.   Further up the road, at a bend before the one
marked 2200m., a jeep track cuts across a saddle behind the
large hillock of Ad. Assaoul (2686m.) to Aguelmous village on
the Sahara side of the Tichka pass. From this bend either take
a good track on to the NE branch of the E ridge and follow up
to summit; or join the same ridge from the saddle (c. 2380m.)
by ascending to pt. 2511m. near junction of the E ridge and its
NE branch, 5 h. from road. All these routes are over distances of 6 to 7 km.

<u>Anrhomer (Anghomar)</u>   3607m. (3610m.)

Most easily approached by the metalled side road just after the
Tichka summit, running to Telouèt (22 km.), then unmade for
13 km. to Anemitèr hamlet. Accommodation possible. Bus
service to Telouèt.   Follow valley due E to where it divides
below the long W ridge of the mountain. Get on to this ridge
by a steep circular movement on its S flank and follow easy
ridge over pt. 3547m. to summit, 7 h. from Anemitèr.

117

Cross country tours Toubkal Region

The classic touring itinerary follows closely below the N side of the main ridge system extending SW to NE, which enables most of the major summits in the region to be climbed as diversions, adding more days to the total time taken; or they can be ignored as inclination, weather and conditions dictate. A second route traverses corresponding ground below the S side of the ridge through altogether more remote country and spartan facilities at the end of day stages; it also presents fewer and tougher opportunities for peak bagging along the way. This route joins the northern one in the upper Ourika valley from where both can be extended to the Tichka pass road.

Many variations to either of these touring routes can be worked out from the map and other descriptions given in the guide. In fact both are infinitely variable.

The N side tour is generally accomplished in 7 days but is possible for fit parties without undue exertion in five, eschewing summiteering ambitions en route. The tour including Toubkal and say three other major summits would occupy at least 12 days.

<u>North Side Tour</u>. Recommended tactics and day stages. For

a leisurely pace, add 50% to times allocated below. Start at Ijoukak on Test pass road in Nfis valley; inns and hut. Carry provisions and gear initially for 3-4 days; one small gas stove per four persons.

1. Hire a lorry or car at Ijoukak to take party up road to El Makhzen mines (1370m.) in Agoundis valley, 8 km. Follow mule trail on L side of Agoundis stream through limestone gorges and picturesque hamlets to Ait Moussa and Aguerda, this last with some huts called Ait Youb beside the stream near the highest cultivations at 1900m., 8 km., $3\frac{1}{2}$ h. Sleeping in Berber hut or house, or camping.

2. The longest and most serious day stage. Axe and crampons useful before end May; axe up to mid July, depending on conditions. From Ait Youb the path continues on L side of stream for 4 km. past various groups of huts to a prominent division in the valley. The N branch goes up to the Tizi Melloul. The main E branch is taken by descending to the stream bed and entering its impressive gorge between black walls where the rocky watercourse and platforms of vegetation are followed for 3 km. to another fork above pt. 2116m. Keep R under a spur, still hugging L side of stream along to where a series of zigzags are seen climbing the S side slopes to the W Zaout pass (2670m.). More of the same work with a rough track in bed for another 2 km. to a large bend where the stream turns N. Cross to the R side, now below the E Zaout pass (2663m.), and continue on this side until the trail coming from latter pass joins the one being followed about 2 km. higher up. One can look back along this trail with its parallel water conduit running to the pass. From this point a rough, steep ascent leads in the main valley N to the Tizi n'Ouagane. After one km. the watercourse is tracked precisely up to pt. 3114m., where the trail goes off up the L side, crossing and ascending bluffs to reach a fairly level upper section in the bed. From the top of this a big scree headwall with rockbands leads to the

col at an average angle of 30°, snow covered until at least mid June; when bare the track is much broken up. So attain the col (3735m.), 7 h. from Ait Youb.

On the other side descend easily to the Neltner hut in 1¼ h. as described under Ouanoukrim normal route.

3. Neltner hut to Imlil. See under Neltner hut, 3 h. on good mule trail.

4. Imlil (q.v.) to Tacheddirt by jeep trail over the Tamatert col (q.v.), 4 h.

5 & 6. At Tacheddirt, two choices for reaching the Upper Ourika valley and Setti Fadma.

Either traverse the Tacheddirt col (q.v.) and descend to Timichi hamlet, 5½ h., in the upper Ourika where a night can be spent before continuing down the long valley trail to Setti Fadma in another 3 h.

Or make a circuit N over the Ouadi (Eddi) pass (q.v.) to Oukaimeden hut, overnight halt, 3½-4 h. To rejoin the upper Ourika next day follow the broad trail from Oukaimeden to the Attar or Ourhens pass (3100m.) above the Tiferguine huts, 2 h., from where a steep zigzag path descends E to Agouns, the highest hamlet in the Ourika, thence to Timichi and the long trail on the N side of the valley to Setti Fadma, another 4½ h.

Continuation to Tichka pass road. This can be done in 2 days, preferably 3, by following routes described in the previous section on Outlying Summits, through the Rhellis depression between Meltsene and the Yagour plateau, stopping at the lower Iferd huts; then by slopes along N foot of Meltsene with a good trail passing through the villages of Addarnane and Quarzazt, followed by a forest descent with jeep road to Azgour and the road in the Zat valley to Ait Slimane, overnight halt. Then by the pastoral trail across the Tizi n'Leilat and down to the Tichka road at Tazlida.

<u>South Side Tour</u>.   This avoids points of comfort such as the Neltner and Oukaimeden huts, Imlil and Tacheddirt.   Altogether, a tougher proposition.

1. As above, to Ait Youb.

2. As for 2 above to the water conduit junction coming from the E Zaout pass. In the main valley mounting N to the Ouagane col you soon cross a branch stream entering from a cwm to the NE, under the Tizi n'Tamrhart (3415m.), a col in the E flanking ridge.   Ascend R side of branch stream over fairly steep and bad scree, mostly trackless, to col at top, easy but tiring. On the other side a rough steep descent to the Ifni lake (2295m.), q.v., about $8\frac{1}{2}$ h. from Ait Youb.

3. Descend main mule trail and jeep road to Amsouzart (1740m.) in the upper Tifnout valley, 2 h.

4. Follow the much used summer mule trail to the Tizi n'Ourai (3109m.), a gentle but long and wearisome ascent of over 1400m., 4 h. On the other side descend by the same trail into the Tifni-Tinzer basin area (q.v.), under Iferouane, to the Likemt or Tinzer huts, $2\frac{1}{2}$ h.

5. The logical exit to the upper Ourika is down the main Tifni river and through the Kassaria gorge system to Tiourdiou village. Difficult route finding and a man with local knowledge is desirable, 5h., plus another $2\frac{1}{2}$ h. down valley to Setti Fadma.

Alternatively, from the Likemt huts cross the Likemt pass (q.v.) to Tacheddirt where the North Side tour route can be joined.

Other zones of the High Atlas

The main range between the Test pass and the Moussa gorges;
the latter are conveniently marked by the S.511 road between
Chichaoua and Agadir. Near the Test pass end the two principal summits of Erdouz and Igdat are described in a previous
section of the guide.
    The western zone has a notably damper climate than the
Toubkal region, being influenced by air currents and moisture
coming from the Atlantic seaboard.   The best inroad to the
Tichka area is the upper Seksaoua valley, reached from Marrakech by the S.511 to Imi n'Tanoute, then by jeep road feasible
for cars to Bou-Laouane and Lalla Aziza in the valley proper.
The highest village with porter services is Aguersaffen. Round
the head of the valley is a remote area, largely uninhabited, of
sharp picturesque summits, complicated in layout and divided
by plateaux linked through passes with poor tracks. The most
conspicuous summit is Ras Moulay Ali (3349m.) with several
pyramid satellites. Tichka itself is a huge plateau escarpment

rising to a maximum elevation in Imaradene (3351m.). Note that the prominent summit of Amendach at E end of this plateau area is wrongly marked on the latest map as 3882; it should read 3382m. While the plateau area itself is of little interest except as a high level walking route along the backbone of the Atlas, peaks rising on spurs to the N and on the continuation of the main ridge SW offer considerable rock climbing potential. These include Tinergouelt (Tinergwet, 3551m.), Aoulime (Awlim, 3482m.), Mtdadene (3366m.), Ikis or Tindri (3183m., no name on map). The best viewpoint for this entire area is Tabgourt (3206m.), which can be reached by walking from a jeep roadhead at the Tabgourt col (2666m.) in $1\frac{1}{2}$ h. The rock of this area is a mixture of limestone, granite, quartzite and schist.

The area can be entered from the W at Argana on the S. 511 by a long jeep road up the Asif n'Ait Dris valley. Accessible jeep roads approach the S side of the crest zone from Taroudannt, from where it is possible to get quite close to the main summits.

CENTRAL HIGH ATLAS

An enormous zone stretching from the Tichka pass road to the Plateau des Lacs, where Imilchil village (2159m.) is the main centre - accessible by a long jeep road - mostly metalled now - from above Beni-Mellal on the P. 24 road.

Irhil M'Goun, highest point called Amsod, 4068m.

The only 4000m. summit of the Atlas chain outside the Toubkal region, and for this reason it has always received attention from peak baggers. Remotely situated as a ridge running for several km. at over 4000m. and forming the most southerly of three parallel ridges comprising this part of the Central High Atlas system. The northerly approach, from Azilal and Ait-Mehammed, offers a rough jeep road over the most northerly ridge barrier into the fertile and populated Bou Goumez valley. After that the central ridge barrier is crossed on foot to reach the long M'Goun ridge. The normal crossing point is the Tizi n'Ait Imi (2910m.), but there are more direct passes. At least two days with camping or bivouac, possibly three, to reach summit. While all the ground is easy the terrain is much contorted and laborious to cross. Epic British ascents in late winter and early spring, involving expedition tactics, are unnecessary in late spring and early summer when snow cover will be adequate to make good progress over the ground in reliable weather conditions. Mule hire and porterage possible in the Bou Goumez valley.

Much the shortest way to climb M'Goun, and possible in three days there and back from Marrakech, is to make an ascent from the south side. A car is essential. Drive to Ouarzazate then Skoura in the Dades valley. From here by jeep road (no. 6831) to Ait Moudzit village, then Tidzguine, directly below the south side of the mountain and some 20 km. distant from the summit. Above the last named village the valley divides; the R (NE) fork is taken directly to foot of mountain, mule hire possible. Ascend one or other of two fairly steep cwms running NE to join the SE ridge of pt. 4014m. Follow up this ridge to latter pt. on the main backbone of M'Goun and continue NE along main ridge for 2 km. to the highest point.

The other big summits in this area, such as Rhat, Tignousti, Azurki and Ouaougoulzat, are generally more accessible from the N (Bou Goumez) side.

Aioui   3382m.

A splendid rock climbing venue, the finest in Morocco and comparable with the best the Dolomites can offer. Reached in 2 h. walking from the village of Zaouia Ahanesal, situated in a cul-de-sac hemmed in by huge escarpments. This village is approached by jeep roads from Ait-Mehammed and Tamda, or directly from Beni-Mellal by the Cathedral Rock road. The N face of the mountain is 4 km. long and at points over 600m. high. The rock is generally sound limestone. About 60 independent route lines have been achieved to date. A summary of over 40 together with a topo-diagram and other information appears in the GHM Annales 1977 (CAF, Paris). More detailed technical descriptions have been published in the same annual dating back to 1958. The easiest routes are grade III, with a normal descent/ascent route of II in a series of gully depressions cutting the E part of the cliffs. Most of the good routes are IV and V, giving up to 700m. of climbing, and several of VI with artificial pitches.

EASTERN HIGH ATLAS

This last section of the main range extends from the Plateau des Lacs (Imilchil) to the Ayachi massif and Midelt. A number of secondary massifs visited from time to time by French parties for spring skiing link the plateau area to the Ayachi; the most important of these is the Masker sub-chain, served by the village of Tounfite (1940m.); roundabout bus service from Midelt.

All the eastern zone is covered by a very detailed up to date guide in French; see bibliography section in Introductory chapter.

<u>Ari n'Ayachi</u> 3747m.

This mountain has knolls similar to M'Goun all of much the same height appearing on a long ridge. The most conspicuous is called Said ou Hadi (3727m.) while the highest point, Ichichi n'Boukhlib (3747m.), is fully 45 min. walking distance E along the main ridge.

From Midelt (1488m., all main services) on the P.21 road, jeep roads are taken along the N side of the massif to reach the usual starting points. The least steep and most pleasant route is also the longest. By car to Tattiouine village (1700m.). From here on muleback to the Ikkis col (2800m.) and thus up again to the main ridge at pt. 3381m. Follow the ridge on foot to summit, altogether about 9 h. from village.

The mountain walking route is started from a camp on the jeep road near Ait Ouchen village (2000m.) and goes up the NW cwm of summit 3727m., directly to the top, about 6 h. Continue E along main ridge to highest point (45 min. - 1 h.).

The scramblers' route, being steeper, starts from a camp on the steep jeep road in the Jaffar cirque (2040m.) on NE side of mountain, and mounts through the Ijimi gorge (good bivouac sites and caves) to a col at the foot of the N ridge of pt. 3727m.; alternatively the latter's NE ridge can be taken with steeper scrambling. Both ridges, steep and rocky but easy, converge below the summit and are cut off by a small gap. One short chimney above the gap is grade II. $5\frac{1}{2}$ h. from roadside camp. Above the Ijimi gorge it is possible to toil straight up long unpleasant gullies towards pt. 3747m. on the main ridge. The best months for an ascent are May and June; then snow cover will be evident above 3300m. At this time the main ridge may still be corniced on N side for several km.

The parallel massif immediately S of the Ayachi is the Maoutfoud, culminating point Sidi Ali ou Abbou (3445m.). Rarely visited.

———

All these zones outside the Toubkal region are without mountain huts and involve using primitive amenities in Berber villages. None of the villages in high valleys have inns, although nearly all base centres mentioned in the notes above now have rooms for visitors set aside in a house by the village chief. The purchase of local foodstuffs in these villages presents no problem, and a remarkable variety of vegetables, fats and meals, and dough products can be found. Apart from home grown produce this is largely due to the current programme of improvement to "pistes" (jeep roads) being carried out by the local and national authorities. Provisions by lorry are brought regularly to remote villages and mountain valley communities.

In these remote zones mountain travellers can often make use of forestry huts (maison forestière, or MF, on maps). Some of these are open and occupied by Berber guardians, others are locked but can be used following inquiry and permission sought at the nearest village. There is a good spirit of co-operation among the Berber people in these matters and the visitor should take particular care not to abuse their hospitality in any way.

Car drivers are warned to carry a spare can containing at least 15 litres of petrol while journeying along piste roads, and always start out for a particular destination or circuit with a full tank. In winter and spring some of these roads may be difficult to negotiate and the fullest inquiries should be made at the nearest township before setting out. Small cars with a high body clearance above the ground are the best vehicles for travelling these roads. In fact the Moroccan authorities state that any ordinary saloon vehicle with an engine capacity greater than 1300cc is unsuitable, always excepting four-wheel drive types. The present writer has used a Renault 4 on many jeep roads in the High Atlas, and has found this vehicle ideal. The smallest Citroën cars are equally good. The British Leyland Mini is unsuitable, being too low-slung, while a Fiat 127 rates somewhere in between. The worst small vehicle, because of negligible ground clearance and poor suspension, is the Ford Fiesta.

Whether or not a party intends to camp or bivouac, equipment for these eventualities should always be taken in reserve. Conditions permitting, mule hire and porter services can nearly always be arranged in high villages, so that loads can be moved up long valley approaches and over passes with suitable trails to enable a party to set up camps near its principal objectives. In general a day rate of Dh. 30.00 for these services applies (in 1979), per mule and its attendant, and again, conditions permitting, Berber tribesmen will accompany parties, or arrange to meet them elsewhere, to assist ongoing movements or evacuation from an area.

With careful planning, and outside the winter season, tactics only slightly more elaborate than those normally used in the Toubkal region at present need be employed to complete climbs and treks successfully in these much less frequented regions of the High Atlas. It should also be noted that the months of July-September inclusive are very arid, hot and tiring, with a frequent problem of finding water.

CARTE DE MAROC 1/100,000

National grid sheets covering the High Atlas between Midelt (E) and the
Moussa gorges (W). Each sheet covers $47\frac{1}{2}$ km. (E-W) x 55 km. (N-S).
On some later editions sheet titles are modified with 'berberised' spellings.

							Midelt
					Imilchil	Tounfite	Rich
		Demnate	Azilal	Zaouia Ahanesal	Tinerhir	Tinejdad	
Imi n'Tanoute	Amizmiz	Oukaimeden Toubkal	Telouèt	Skoura	El Kelâa des Mgouna	Boumalne	
Igli	Tizi n'Test	Taliwine	Tazenakht				

Four 1/50,000 maps divide each 1/100,000 sheet equally.

Index